D1248002

LOUISIANIANS ALL

by Jeanne Frois

Illustrated by Nathan B. Carley

PELICAN PUBLISHING COMPANY
GRETNA 1992

The word "Pelican" and the depiction of a pelican are trademarks of Pelican Publishing Company, Inc., and are registered in the U.S. Patent and Trademark office.

Library of Congress Cataloging-in-Publication Data

Frois, Jeanne.
    Louisianians all / by Jeanne Frois.
        p.   cm.
    Includes bibliographical references.
    Summary: Biographies of famous Louisianians who helped shape their state's history. Includes Huey Long, Lafcadio Hearn, Louis Armstrong, and Henry Shreve.
    ISBN 0-88289-824-8
    1. Louisiana—Biography—Juvenile literature.
2. Louisiana—History—Juvenile literature. [1. Louisiana— Biography.   2. Louisiana—History.]   I. Title.
CT237.F76   1992
976.3'0099—dc20   92-19208
[B]   CIP
                                                          AC

Manufactured in the United States of America.

Published by Pelican Publishing Company, Inc.
1101 Monroe Street, Gretna, Louisiana 70053

In loving and grateful dedication to my parents:
Cyril, my father (in memory),
and Etta, my mother.

CONTENTS

PREFACE

When Pelican Publishing Company offered me the opportunity to write a biographical book for Louisiana's schoolchildren, with the goal of introducing them to the heritage of our state, I felt it was a concept that had long been needed. For Louisiana has a noble facet to its history, worthy of its children's pride.

Although the people I've selected to include in this book represent the many different cultures that migrated to Louisiana, their stories give witness to one common denominator: the triumphant human spirit that is within all of us.

Now that *Louisianians All* is completed and I look at the list of names of the people whose history I've recorded, I feel as if I'm looking over the names of dear friends I've come to know. Learning about their lives was a source of inspiration for myself. I humbly hope that, by telling their stories to young people, I have somehow contributed to the legacy these remarkable people hoped to leave the generations of Louisianians who would follow them.

Here, then, is their story.

JEANNE FROIS
Metairie, Louisiana

ACKNOWLEDGMENTS

I would like to express my deep appreciation to the following people who assisted me during the writing of this book:

To my mother, Etta, for being a supporting sounding board and critic.

To my brother, Tim, and his wife, Patricia.

To the Louisiana History Department of the University of New Orleans for helping to clarify miscellaneous data.

To James McAllister, a student worker at the University of New Orleans' Earl K. Long Library, for his invaluable help among the stacks of the Louisiana section.

To the staff of the Louisiana section of the New Orleans Public Library's main branch.

To the Public Relations Office of the New York Yankees baseball team for providing me with a history of Ron Guidry's career.

To Diane Armstrong of Typing Plus for her expert computer input of the manuscript, especially when the deadline crunch was upon me.

Special thanks to the "Archangel," whose love was so much a part of this book.

LOUISIANIANS ALL

CHARLES P. ADAMS

HE WAS A GENTLE GIANT of a man, six feet, ten inches tall. He was strong and hard enough to break the ground with a plow, gentle and patient enough to plant seeds and watch over them like a good parent and await their growth. He was a farmer and a teacher. He gave his students the same patient devotion he gave to his fields. From the minds of young black people, he drew their potential and helped it flower. He placed all of his own personal dreams aside to achieve this objective and gave blacks their first school of higher learning in Louisiana: Grambling State University.

His grandmother was Mariah, a slave from Virginia who was sold to a Louisiana planter named Jim Wood. Mariah became the cook for the household of her new owner. She had eight children, one of whom was Mary, the mother of Charles Adams. The Civil War freed Mariah of slavery and allowed her to go anywhere she desired. She gathered up her eight children and left the plantation. Through hard work, she was able to buy thirty acres of land. She was a strong woman respected by both the black and white people of her community.

Her daughter, Mary, married Edward Adams. They earned their living as sharecroppers on a small plantation in Brusly, Louisiana, in West Baton Rouge Parish, where Charles was born in 1873. When he was a very young child, a can of oil was left too near a hearth fire and exploded. His young mother and smaller brother were killed. When their father remarried, the three remaining children of Mary went to live with Mariah.

Grandmother Mariah put Charles to work. He helped tend the farm with his two uncles. He learned how to plow and sow seeds. He learned respect for the earth and the farm animals who helped his family so much in their work. In the fields, he also learned patience.

When Charles was nineteen, he and Uncle William offered a down payment of five hundred dollars for the purchase of a hundred acres of land near the Mississippi River. He owned his own farm, four hundred barrels of corn, and two mules worth five hundred dollars each.

While Charles had been learning farming, one of his aunts had been teaching him simple arithmetic, reading, and writing. Happy as he was at farming, Charles wanted to achieve something more. His dream was to attend college and become a lawyer. When he was twenty-three years old, he heard about a school in Alabama for black people called Tuskegee Institute. It was founded by a trailblazer for the advancement of black people, Booker T. Washington.

With his family thinking him insane for giving up farming, Charles left them in November 1896 and showed up at the gates of Tuskegee. Charles was first placed in the slowest classes, then worked himself into the highest ranking classes in all of his subjects. Charles joined Tuskegee's debating society. Asked to give an address, Charles spoke of his life in rural Louisiana, his farm, and the seasons of seed and harvest, of searching the sky each day for sunlight and rain, entreating both to fall on his fields in equal measure.

Charles became Tuskegee's best debater and represented his school in tournaments with other institutions.

He was older than the rest of the students. They looked up to him as an affectionate and wise older brother, and brought all their problems to his willing ear and big heart. He supported himself by first carrying wood to the brick yard, cleaning the boys' dormitory, and by bookkeeping for the school and for a campus livery stable. And Charles found both a friend and supporter in the school's principal, Booker T. Washington. In May of 1901, Washington told Charles that there were plans for an industrial school similar to Tuskegee to be founded and built in North Louisiana. Someone was needed to carry out this plan, and Washington told Charles he was the perfect person to accomplish this task. Booker T. Washington told him he was needed by the black people who had to be educated if their standard of life in the South would ever be improved. Charles was convinced and gave up his plans to study law. Washington, who once said, "I will not permit any man to narrow and degrade my soul by making me hate him," urged Charles to work with all men, including white men, because all people need one another. He further advised the student body of 1901 when they returned home better educated than their parents, not to think they were better than anyone because they had more schooling.

After graduation, Charles journeyed to North Louisiana to the proposed site of the school, which was a thick forest of pine and gum trees. Without receiving any pay, he traveled hilly North Louisiana by any means available: horseback, wagon, and his own feet. He visited black communities and churches spreading the word about the intended school and asking for students to join. The founding of what would be Grambling State University began. The building was constructed much in the manner of a barn raising by the help of the farmers and their families.

On November 1, 1901, with 125 students and three teachers the Colored Industrial and Agricultural School was formally opened. Tuition was five dollars a month. Most of the students had no cash. The cost of their schooling was paid by offering sacks of potatoes, peas, or flour, or other useful items handmade by the students' families.

The younger students were taught how to read, write, and calculate, with instructions on cleanliness and citizenship. The older students were taught farming, animal husbandry, and how to buy property. They also learned home remedies for illnesses to keep their families healthy. That first year found Charles dealing with the struggle of keeping his school. He fought an attempt of a takeover by black Baptists who wanted to turn the school into a seminary. Despite its problems that first year, the Colored Industrial and Agricultural School grew.

Miss Lidelia Jewett and Dr. Lillian Martin, two white ladies from San Francisco, visited the school and were impressed by its work. Along with wealthy Northern people, they gave money to Charles to help the school.

A young woman named Martha Adams was a teacher at the school. Brisk, pretty, filled with energy, she taught the young women sewing, cooking, and handicraft. She and Charles fell in love and were married in May 1905.

In 1914, the institution became known as the Allen Green–Grambling Consolidated Industrial High School after merging with another school.

Through the next two decades, Charles struggled to keep the school afloat. By 1928, the Lincoln Parish school board told him they could no longer pay the salaries of the teachers. The school would close without teachers. If Charles could get the school named a state institution, his money problems would disappear.

It was an election year. When Huey P. Long was elected governor, Charles enlisted the aid of Lincoln Parish senator R. P. Knott, who approved of the school.

Charles and Senator Knott met the new governor in his Shreveport office, and the senator presented Charles' idea of turning the school into a state institution. Governor Long told them there was no money for such a project. Charles sat silently through most of the meeting. And then, the former star debater of Tuskegee saw his chance to speak. He spoke only once sentence, telling Governor Long that if he didn't help the black people of Northern Louisiana, then nothing would *ever* be done for them. The simplicity and truth of his words reached Huey P. Long. Unknown to Charles, the new governor was a tremendous admirer of Booker T. Washington. He was impressed to learn that Charles had studied under him and had gone to Grambling on Washington's recommendation.

Huey Long gave Senator Knott permission to introduce the bill to make the Grambling school a state institution at the next legislative session and pledged his support. He signed the bill in July 1928. The school was given still another name: The Louisiana Negro Normal and Industrial School. Under the improved flow of funds, the institution survived.

When Governor Long was killed by an assassin's bullet in 1935, Charles Adams and the Louisiana Negro Normal and Industrial School lost a good friend. No sooner had Long died than the state superintendent of schools, T. H. Harris, a longtime enemy of Charles' and the school's, began a hateful campaign that would force Charles into retirement at age sixty-two.

After years of struggling and self-sacrifice for his school, Charles gave up his presidency. He taught for one year in high school. The rest of his life was spent involved in church work and public speaking. He died at the age of eighty-eight in 1961.

But his industrial school that he lovingly nurtured to suit the educational needs of his race in turn-of-the-century Louisiana remains. As the years brought the need for advancement in teaching to help black people go forward in the world, so changed the Louisiana Negro Normal and Industrial School. In 1946, it became known simply as Grambling State University. It has brought about scholastic achievement and has given the world many fine teachers, doctors, lawyers, artists, and athletes. It has become a symbol of excellence in achievement for black people.

It was Charles Adams' finest harvest.

LOUIS ARMSTRONG

. . . *Gabriel's trumpet*

IT WAS A MOVIE set in the early 1930s. A short feature was being filmed of a black orchestra standing waist-high in soap bubbles. Its smiling-faced leader, Louis Armstrong, was ordered by the studio to appear in the film wearing a leopard-skin suit while he sang a song making fun of his dark skin and "kinky" hair. It could have been a scene of cruel, racial ridicule put together by white producers to get laughs at the black man's expense. But the bandleader was Louis Armtrong, master trumpeter. The brilliance of his horn playing and talent for comedy made him shine with the dignity that goes with genius. In what could have been a most undignified scene, there were few people who possessed more dignity than he did at that moment. It seemed he was laughing at the producer for paying him to be in such a ridiculous scene, and he played it to the hilt. It was the kind of spirit that made Louis Armstrong a hero to the black people of his time, and had the entire world eating out of his hand.

He always claimed that he was born July 4, 1900, and was an All-American baby, but the baptismal records of Sacred Heart of Jesus Church on Canal Street in New Orleans say he was really born August 4, 1901. His father deserted him, and Louis was very close to his mother Mayann. Louis grew up in Storyville, a notorious district of New Orleans. It was an area filled with honky-tonk barrooms from which came the sound of a raw, sassy music that would become known as jazz. The sounds of a tinny piano being played, banjos thumbing to a driving rhythm, and the belting voice of a trumpet spilled out into the streets of Storyville. Robbers, drunkards, murderers, and the women of Basin Street were part of Louis' environment as a boy. But his family was close-knit, even if it was dirt-poor, his mother devoted, and her son was a good child.

Befriended by a white Jewish family, Louis went to work alongside their son delivering coal to the many women who lived in Storyville. The Jewish family often invited young Louis to their home for dinner and taught him to sing lullabies. He loved music and when he had saved enough money from his wages, he bought himself a coronet. Teaching himself to play, Louis still longed for proper lessons. He got his wish, but not in the way he would have liked. One New Years Eve, when he was small, people of his neighborhood were lighting firecrackers in the street. Louis borrowed someone's gun, and in the spirit of celebration, began lighting his own firecrackers by firing the gun at them. Promptly arrested, he was carted off to a reform school called the Colored Waif's Home. The music teacher there recognized his talent, and began teaching him to blow the bugle, showing him how to properly hold his lips while playing the horn. When he left the Waif's Home, Louis returned to Storyville, where trumpeter Joe Oliver, who became known as the immortal "King Oliver," schooled Louis further in trumpet playing while Mrs. Oliver fed Louis red beans and rice.

In 1918, when King Oliver left the severe racial oppression that was in New Orleans at that time for Chicago, Louis became the lead trumpeter of the Crescent City. He played weddings, dances, picnics, and on riverboats. His reputation spread as far as Idaho. King Oliver sent for Louis to join his band in Chicago as second trumpeter. Louis surpassed even

King Oliver and went on to form his own bands known as the Hot Five and the Hot Seven. They began recording songs called "Gully Low Blues" and "Potato Head Blues." The popularity of his music grew. His trumpet playing was perfection, his gravelly voice told a story as he sang. All of the years of being a black man who had to keep a respectful silence burst into the expression of his music and the notes he composed on his horn.

Once during a recording session, Louis dropped the sheet music that had the lyrics he was singing printed on it. Rather than ruin the "take," he began singing the sounds, "Ree-bop, dee-dop, dee-dop, dee-boom" in perfect time to the music. It sounded wonderful, the producers allowed it to stay in the song, and the record was a hit. Thus, Louis had instituted the old custom used by black New Orleans jazz players called "scatting" into the tradition of jazz music.

Throughout the thirties, forties and fifties, he became an international star who entertained royalty and who starred in movies. In the early days of his fame, he was called "Satchel Mouth" by his fellow musicians because of his large mouth and belting voice. When he went to perform in Great Britain, the English press shortened the nickname to "Satchmo," and thus, he was forever known. Europeans adored him.

He once returned to New Orleans, an international star, to play at a concert that would also be broadcast over the radio. The announcer, a white man, refused to introduce the black Louis. Flashing his big warm grin, Louis walked up to the microphone, announced himself, and led his band into its opening number.

A man who never had a Christmas tree until he was nearly forty years old and who sat for hours watching it with the wide eyes of a child, Louis became a bona fide, certified celebrity of Hollywood. In 1964, he had the number one record in the nation with his rendition of "Hello Dolly," a tune from the Broadway play.

He was, and still is, considered to be the American genius who took the jazz music of the black man and elevated it to an art form. From Satchmo's influence on jazz and blues, rock and roll evolved.

He made the cover of *Time* magazine, and popular *Life* magazine wrote an article about his life. He traveled all over the world during the length of his career, and the public never stopped loving the music and warm enormous smiles of this most gracious man. He was often called America's goodwill ambassador to the world.

In July of 1971, after a long illness, Louis Armstrong died. His funeral in New York was televised nationally, the president of the United States made a public statement of mourning, and the honorary pallbearers at his memorial service included Frank Sinatra, Ella Fitzgerald, Pearl Bailey, Johnny Carson, and Dizzy Gillespie. The entire world mourned Louis Armstrong's passing.

When disk jockey Fred Robbins was nearly finished eulogizing Satchmo, he looked heavenward and addressed the archangel Gabriel, who is, they say, God's celestial trumpeter.

"Move over, Gabriel," he advised, "Satchmo's coming."

CAPT. LEVIERRE COOLEY

. . . friendly passage

BORN IN SAVANNAH, ILLINOIS, in 1853, Levierre V. Cooley lived on the banks of the Mississippi
River. It was the glory days of the steamboat, and the
river was filled with these vessels. Growing up on the
river, young Levierre heard the haunting and soulful
bass sound of the steamboats' horns as they rounded
the bends in the river. He thrilled to the sound which
vibrated in his chest and tingled in his ears. It seemed
to be calling to him, and the long charcoal streaks of
smoke from the smokestacks that trailed behind the
riverboats, seemed to be fingers that beckoned to him
to follow. Watching the paddlewheels at the back of
the boats as they turned the river into waterfalls,
Levierre vowed that one day he would be a riverboat
pilot.

When he was fourteen, he took a step toward
achieving this dream by working on a steamboat. The
river became his life. He both worked and lived on it,
hauling and loading cargo. By the time he had grown
into a strong, powerfully built man, he was the owner
of numerous riverboat "packets," or boats that carried
cargo and other goods on a regular schedule. When
he married, he, his wife, and their daughter Sophie
lived on the *Ouachita,* his favorite packet boat.

From his base in both southern Arkansas and
northern Louisiana, Levierre carried mail and goods
on fixed routes through the four major rivers of
Louisiana: the Mississippi, the Red, the Black, and the
Ouachita. Up and down these rivers he traveled, until
he came to know every creek, eddy, and sandbar. His
weatherbeaten face with its full moustache became

familiar as he drifted through the heartland of the state. He became steeped in the knowledge of its people—the black roustabouts working his ships, the women in shantyboat houses on river banks who watched as he passed, their many children beside them. He saw single candles burning in cabin windows under night skies filled with stars. He passed the glorious Gothic passenger steamboats, looking like wedding cakes on frothy coffee-colored waters. And he passed the high-columned mansions of the Southern gentry crumbling into decay after the Civil War. His view changed every minute as the boat which was both his home and livelihood, forever moved through four rivers. He brought comforts to the points at which he stopped: long-awaited letters from loved ones, a bolt of cloth for a young woman's wedding dress, and other simple, everyday things that were so important.

His kindliness, dependability, and warmth made him well known and loved by everyone he met. He became a legend on the river. He listened to stories of people's hardships and triumphs, as well as the folklore and tall tales spun by the black boat workers and the river people living on the banks.

The fame of his hearty personality spread.

Journalists and novelists came to consult with him, to hear him tell the rich tales his life on the river had given him. Many of his stories were used by writers in novels and magazine articles. He became known as the "grand old man of the river."

From the top of the state to the bottom, Captain Cooley continued to make his river passages, which were more like goodwill excursions than cargo drops, until December 1931. While he was on the Ouachita River, he was stricken by an attack of the heart disease that had plagued him for some time. When his boat docked at New Orleans on December 9, he was rushed to Southern Baptist Hospital. He died on a Saturday afternoon five days before Christmas.

Capt. Levierre V. Cooley wrote no masterpieces, made no medical breakthroughs, and never revolutionized the shipping industry.

He was a river master, but that was only because he had made friends with the ways of the river and bowed his head in respect to its wishes. He was a master navigator so he could better serve people. And he knew the human spirit and respected human dignity. He was a man whom everyone could consistently rely upon, a folk hero who linked the people of the state through his kindly travels and by simply doing his work well.

When the news of his death spread from New Orleans to the north of the state, many people gathered to mourn. The banks of the four rivers he had navigated were lined with mourners brought together to pay tribute to the mighty river master who had also been their friend.

ETIENNE DE BORE

ONE EVENING WHEN THE SUN was setting in a red and purple blaze, Etienne de Boré, instead of having his supper, went for a walk along the grounds of his plantation until he reached the banks of the river. There he stood, deep in thought.

He was so weary of it: having to depend on growing indigo for his living, a crop that had grown to be so—undependable. The blue-flowered indigo plant had made many a Louisiana settler wealthy, but it was now draining the soil of its richness, turning it into an anemic mess that could no longer support plant life. The favorite meal of the grasshopper, indigo was also unable to survive the high winds and fogs that chose to visit Louisiana often in that Year of Our Lord, 1795. Their staple crop had failed Louisianians, and the future that loomed ahead seemed to promise nothing but empty fields that meant bleak poverty.

He was weary of that as well—worrying about the future. Worry wouldn't magically plant a bumper crop in his fields that would make him an ever richer man. Worry, like indigo, must also fall by the wayside. Let his fellow planters moan and wail about their bad luck. He was Jean Etienne de Boré, descended from French nobility in the Northern district of France. His ancestors had held high-ranking positions in the courts of French kings, from one generation to the next. *He* was not going under without a fight.

Etienne (a French name meaning Stephen) was born in the Louisiana province in the area which is now Illinois. Born two days after Christmas in 1741,

Etienne spent the first four years of his life in America. His parents then took him to France.

As he grew into young manhood in France, he was a member of the King's Troops that only the blue bloods of nobility could join, and became the commander of a cavalry company. He married the daughter of Jean-Baptiste Destrehan, an heiress who owned a great deal of land in Louisiana. They returned to the Louisiana Province and made their home on a plantation. Their acres adjoined the old Foucher plantation, which is now the site of Audubon Park.

As he stood that evening watching the river, his thoughts raced onward. He had had a prosperous, satisfying life in South Louisiana, and he intended to keep it that way. Never mind that he was fifty-four years old, an age when people, especially the young, tell you it's time to retire and gracefully take whatever life hands you. *Another* more reliable, staple crop was needed for Louisiana. Etienne's memory began to stir.

Back in 1764, Chevalier de Masan had sold his plantation to Etienne's father, Louis. De Masan had tried to grow acres of sugarcane, a crop the French-Canadian explorer Iberville had brought from Santo Domingo to Louisiana in 1700. Attempts to grow it in Louisiana usually failed. Even the green-thumbed Jesuit priests had been unable to succeed. The sugarcane plant, native to southeastern Asia, had been cultivated successfully in the Central and South Americas since the sixteenth century by European settlers who knew what they were doing. As far back as the early 1300s, Venice, Italy, had been the center of sugar refinery in Europe. But in 1764, even Louis de Boré's crop had failed. In Louisiana, getting the plant to live to harvest time was difficult; refining its syrup to the granulated state of sugar had been next to impossible.

But in 1795, Etienne realized that he had at his disposal the one thing sugarcane planters in Louisiana never had before: experts. He knew of an Antoine Morin, a sugar grower who had lived in the West Indies. In 1791, a violent slave revolt had erupted. Armed with machetes and other weapons, the slaves had attacked white planters and their families and massacred them. Only the personal devotion of his own valet helped Morin escape the West Indies by night. Along with other sugar growers, Antoine Morin came to Louisiana. Sugar making had been a thriving business in the Caribbean, and men who had mastered its art were now in Louisiana.

And the syrup ground from the cane would yield still another product. The Louisiana French called it *tafia* but the English called it rum.

That year, Etienne risked his entire fortune to turn his lands into a sugar plantation. His acres were planted with cane that grew as tall as a man. His fields were filled with the long, thin stalks and their fan-like leaves that waved wildly in the wind. Under the guidance of Antoine Morin, Etienne tended to his crop. Neighbors, relatives, and even strangers went to him and begged him to give up his foolhardy enterprise. He politely thanked them for their advice and then ignored them.

When his crop was harvested and the cane stripped of its leaves, so that it resembled a bamboo fishing pole, it was brought to the sugar house he had built. On that fateful day, cane was fed into a mill that had large wooden wheels. The wheels were turned by tied animals walking round and round the mill in circles. This device crushed the cane plant until the syrup ran from the juicy stalks. Joining Etienne, Antoine Morin and the slaves, were many of Etienne's neighbors, gathered to see either success or failure. The atmosphere was heavy with suspense. As the crushed cane made syrup, the liquid ran down a gutter-like sluice into a huge, black iron cauldron. There it would be boiled over roaring wood fires that could never be allowed to go out, night or day, until the syrup reached the grainy state of sugar. A wonderful candy-like smell floated on the air as the sweet syrup churned in the cauldrons for hours. Suddenly the people gathered to watch the boiling process heard a cry: "IT GRANULATES!" A bowl was scooped into the kettle and then handed to Etienne. The bowl was filled with a gritty brown substance that resembled damp river sand. Dipping his fingers into it, he sampled what must have been the most delicious sugar he'd ever tasted.

He made twelve thousand dollars profit on his crop that year. Other Louisiana planters followed Etienne's example and became sugar growers and wealthy men. The economy of Louisiana was not only rescued, it became downright fat. In 1803, when Spain transferred Louisiana to France, a most respected and much-praised Etienne was made the mayor of New Orleans.

Although sometimes he has mistakenly been called the first man ever to make sugar in history, had it not been for his courage, vision, and leadership, Louisiana would not be ranked today as one of the foremost sugar producers in the world.

On the plantation that had played such a leading role in changing the course of Louisiana's future, Jean Etienne de Boré died. He was seventy-nine years old.

BERNARDO DE GALVEZ

. . . I alone

WITH MERRY, GOOD-NATURED EYES, he was as round and chubby as the pigeons that perched on the rooftop corners of the Cabildo. He looked like a quiet colonial shopkeeper or bookkeeper instead of a blazing hero of the high seas, or the governor of a territory.

Bernardo de Gálvez was born in 1746 in a Spanish village called Macharaviaya. His family was of the nobility of Spain but had lost their wealth. Their poverty did not dampen their sense of loyalty to their country. Bernardo's father, Matias, was an appointed viceroy of Mexico. His uncle José served as secretary of state and president of the council that governed Spanish interest pertaining to the Indies. And young Bernardo began his service to Spain when he was but sixteen as a cadet of the Walloon guards. By the time he was twenty, Bernardo was a comrade-in-arms with Alexander O'Reilly, a man who became the second governor of Louisiana when it was but a province. As governor, O'Reilly established the *Cabildo* (council) as a means to set up Spanish laws in Louisiana. By the time Luis Unzaga became governor in 1769, with twenty-nine-year-old Bernardo as his colonel, Louisiana was beginning to progress under the wise Spanish rule. But by 1776, one large problem loomed on the horizon: the American Revolution and the British who had control of Baton Rouge, Mobile, and Pensacola. The British territory of West Florida reached from Natchez to Lake Pontchartrain, and from the Mississippi River to the Appalachicola River. Unzaga feared that the empire-hungry, scarlet-coated British

39

had their sights set on the desirable jewel of the Mississippi River that was New Orleans. From a military standpoint, Louisiana was in no position to defend itself should this become necessary. Governor Unzaga had no wish to tread on the Redcoats' toes and stir up their instinct for conquest. Yet, despite his caution, he still sold ten thousand pounds of Spanish gunpowder to the American colonists who wanted independence from England. When Unzaga was named captain general of Caracas, Venezuela, thirty-year-old Bernardo de Gálvez became governor of the Louisiana province in 1777.

While the older Unzaga had been careful not to offend the British, young Bernardo all but thumbed his nose in their faces. He ran up a flag of support for liberty and independence for all the world to see—especially the British. Ignoring British complaints, he gave safe harbor to American ships in Louisiana's ports. He helped the struggling new nation's war effort by providing it with guns and ammunition. Oliver Pollock, the agent for the American government, received money and credit secretly from Bernardo, who also had the secret approval of the Spanish throne to help the Americans. When British ships were discovered carrying illegal goods in Louisiana waters, Bernardo most happily had the ships seized.

For the next two years, the young governor repeatedly tweaked the noses of the British by helping the Americans. In 1779, Bernardo's mother country, Spain, joined the Americans and French in what was beginning to look like a club of nations who were forced to declare war on Great Britain. Bernardo responded to the news with the speed of a ball shot from a cannon. Recruiting civilians to add to the state militia and Spanish troops, he made preparations to drive the redcoats out of Baton Rouge. Even a hurricane that destroyed his fleet of boats did not stop Bernardo. Instead of sailing up the river to Baton Rouge, he and his fourteen hundred troops marched overland to the strong British fort. To trick the English soldiers, Bernardo ordered some of his own men into a mosquito-infested forest during the night. He commanded them to begin firing on the British as a distraction. While his men in the forest kept the British occupied, Bernardo cleverly slipped his cannons into key position. It was September 21, 1779. Three hours after the Louisianians began bombardment of the fort, the British admitted that they were defeated. Included in the terms of surrender was Bernardo's demand that they also leave Natchez. His victory that day played a major role in completely removing the British from the vital waterway that was the Mississippi. Bernardo, generous of girth, was also a military dynamo.

But the English still had possession of Mobile and Pensacola. From the Spanish leaders in Havana, Cuba, Bernardo received a signal to attack both Mobile and Pensacola. Organizing a fleet of twelve vessels, Bernardo and his 750 troops slipped into Mobile Bay and laid siege to the British stronghold. By March 1780, the British had again surrendered to Bernardo.

Seven months later, Bernardo, whose motto it seemed was "why quit when you're ahead?" sailed to Havana with an idea to cause further grief for the British. He wanted Pensacola. He received support for his plan from the Spanish government in the form of a fleet and four thousand men. But another hurricane would scatter his fleet as far away as New Orleans and Campeche. Neither the sea nor the wind would sway Bernardo from his purpose. He gathered a smaller group of soldiers, slightly more than thirteen

hundred strong, and sailed to the sparkling aqua-
marine waters of Pensacola, where the beaches
seemed to be made of white sugar instead of plain
sand. He captured Santa Rosa Island, but at the entrance to Pensacola Bay one of his ships ran aground
on a sandbar. The commander of the Spanish fleet,
separate in authority from Bernardo, would not allow
his own ships to sail into the bay. Bernardo's own sailing pilot inspected the area and declared that the
ships could get through. Bernardo commanded his
Louisiana ships to sail. As they progressed in a swell-
ing, graceful line across the treacherous bar, the
sound of cheering from the sailors left behind traveled over the bay. For this bravery, Bernardo received
royal acclaim, and the phrase "Yo solo" ("I alone") was
added to his coat of arms. Once again, the British
surrendered on May 10, 1781. With the loss of Pensacola, the English also lost the entire British territory
of West Florida. When it was time to receive the British surrender, no sun-bronzed, handsomely thin field
marshall with romantically torn clothes emerged
from the Spanish fleet. Instead came Bernardo,
round, portly with a receding hairline, gentle of manner, with the fire of victory in his eyes. Bernardo's
conquests on the Gulf Coast and in Louisiana greatly
helped to secure American independence for the
New England colonists.

While he was helping to win a new nation, Bernardo never neglected his duties as governor of Louisiana. Improving the laws of the province, he also
promoted and sold the many crops grown in the
bounty that was Louisiana. He further assisted the
economy and commerce of the territory by supporting the growth of tobacco and indigo crops. Indigo
was a highly valued plant because it produced a beautiful blue dye the color of the sky at twilight. His

tolerance for humanity also laid the cornerstone that made Louisiana attractive to people of all nations to migrate to and make their home. He brought settlers from the Canary Islands, gave them homes and livestock, while also soothing the tensions between the French and Spanish. He won the everlasting regard of the Indians because he insisted that white people uphold fair trading practices with them.

Bernardo left Louisiana to succeed his father in Mexico as viceroy. In 1786, he died of yellow fever in Mexico City at the age of forty. His short life had been one of adventure, victory, and humanitarianism. When he died, he left an established new nation he had helped create and a stable Louisiana. Now, it was time for him to take another voyage, an adventure of a different kind.

CHARLES GAYARRE

. . . *"rage against the dying of the light"*

HE WAS BORN in January, five years after the turn of the nineteenth century. His great-grandfather had journeyed from Spain to Louisiana with Gov. Antonio de Ulloa, the first Spanish governor of Louisiana, in the eighteenth century. They arrived in a territory where the people were die-hard French in their loyalties. When Governor Ulloa was driven out of New Orleans by a rebellion, Don Esteban Gayarré remained as loyal comptroller and commissary. Don Esteban's son, Antonio, served with another Louisiana governor, Gálvez, and the two fought side by side against the British in West Florida. Antonio married the daughter of Etienne de Boré, a planter who experimented with what was then the little-known art of making sugar. He successfully fathered Louisiana's sugar industry. His grandson was Charles Etienne Arthur Gayarré.

Charles spent his childhood on his grandfather de Boré's plantation on the banks of the Mississippi River. He was educated at a country school begun by other wealthy planters.

By the time Charles had turned twenty in 1825, he graduated from the College d'Orleans.

Charles was a serious young man in whom fairness and reason were balanced. He had the romantic face of a Spaniard, part conquistador, part pirate. He journeyed to Philadelphia and for three years was a student of a celebrated expert in law, William Rawles. He began his own legal career in New Orleans at the age of twenty-three. Two years later, he was elected to the lower house of the Louisiana state senate. When

45

his term had ended, Charles was appointed presiding judge of the city court of New Orleans *and* assistant attorney general of Louisiana. When he was but three days past his thirtieth birthday, the young man was elected United States senator. He had labored constantly for most of his young manhood, and exhaustion overcame him. He collapsed from illness. His burned-out condition forced him to resign his senate seat and sent him on a trip abroad that would last eight years. Yet the proud and disciplined Charles did not waste away his time in France; instead, he wrote a book, the first book in a series of volumes that would tell the history of Louisiana.

Unpressured by the duties of state office, this history lover delved into the abundant material housed in the French archives. He unraveled the mysteries of the state's origins amid papers, parchments, and documents once sealed with wax and signed by beringed hands above which had risen lace cuffs and satin sleeves. He read and searched and scribbled, always seeking the knowledge that would piece together and bring alive Louisiana's past and reveal to her people their heritage for all generations. A true researcher, in any field, is part scholar, part detective, and part drudge, and Charles balanced all of these traits within himself to write *Histoire de la Louisiane*. Charles petitioned Gov. Alexander Mouton to purchase sets of the original French documents pertaining to Louisiana from France. As a result, the valued documents were brought home to Louisiana. They remain in the state to this day.

After eight years abroad, Charles returned home in 1843. He ended thirty-eight years of bachelorhood by marrying the widowed Annie Buchanan of Jackson, Mississippi, and continued writing the history of Louisiana. Three years later, 1846, would be a banner year for Charles. *Histoire de la Louisiane,* Volume I, would be published and Gov. Isaac Johnson would name him secretary of state.

The long-standing tradition of Louisiana's dishonest political machinery was planting its seeds during Charles' lifetime. In 1853, John Slidell defeated him in a race for Congress. Charles, his legal blood boiling and his researcher's nose itching to find out the facts and get to the truth, presented sound proof that a third of the votes cast in the election were fake. Perhaps had Charles not possessed the popularity and support of the public before the election, he would have accepted his defeat without question. Despite Charles' evidence, Slidell kept the seat he "won" in Congress. Charles was inspired to write *The School of Politics,* a novel that made fun of crooked political practices.

In 1854, Volume II of *Histoire de la Louisiane* was completed, and told the story of the Spanish domination of the state.

Inability to turn against his home state caused Charles to support the Confederacy even as his intelligence and reason made him realize the hopelessness of the Southern Cause. He weathered the War Between the States and the Yankee occupation of New Orleans by writing the third volume of his history of Louisiana, documenting the period under the American flag. When it was published in 1866, Charles was a man ruined by the defeat of the south. His large fortune was lost. It was the time of the Reconstruction, the Old South was dead, and Charles was growing old. He tried to earn a living by writing, but he and Annie slowly slid downhill into poverty. They lost a country home named Roncal, and moved into a cramped house on Prieur Street. One by one, they sold their possessions to survive. Yet, living in almost

47

desperate poverty, Charles still wrote constantly. He penned a psychological study of Philip of Spain, and two novels, *Aubert Duboyet,* or *The Two Republics,* and *Fernando de Lemos, Truth and Fiction.* He served as reporter of the decisions of the Louisiana Supreme Court for three years, and president of the Louisiana Historical Society for twenty-eight years. He and Annie maintained a close friendship with Grace King, whom they regarded as a daughter. But for the most part, Charles was overlooked. Innovativeness and courage had been passed to him by his ancestors: There was still so much he was able to contribute. He was not one to take kindly to being put out to pasture, as unfortunately was, and sometimes still is, the attitude of people toward the elderly. His writings still maintained the ability to awaken the past and allow it to play as vividly as the present in the reader's imagination; his own mind was still rapier-sharp. Yet people forget that one day, they, too, will be old, and the slowing of the body does not always mean that the mind and spirit falter, nor that the feelings of youth die.

Charles Gayarré died at the age of ninety, penniless, but not broken. And he bequeathed a most valuable legacy to a people who seemed to have forgotten him. He gave to Louisiana its own story, as wide and sweeping as the river which mothered her. He helped Louisiana find her true identity—Bienville, Indians, indigo, sugarcane, pirates, noblemen, New Englanders, French dandies, Africans—all the influences of the settlers whose blood lives on to this day through their descendants he set down in ink and recorded it for all time. He was a preservationist and, to this day, professors still consider *Histoire de la Louisiane* the Bible of Louisiana history.

Nearly fifty years after Charles' death, Dylan Thomas, a young Welsh poet, wrote some lines pertaining to death and old age:

Do not go gentle into that good night,
Rage, rage against the dying of the light.

Charles Gayarré would have agreed.

RON GUIDRY

HE WAS A SKINNY, spindly armed young pitcher who seemed too frail for major league baseball. He had a shock of dark hair, eyes just as dark, a moustache, and his voice was rich with the accent of Acadia where he was born. His French ancestors had been cruelly expelled from Nova Scotia, Canada, by the British in 1755. Herded onto ships with no destination except any port that would welcome them, these Acadians, or "Cajuns" as they were called, finally arrived in Southern Louisiana and settled in the area of Lafayette. Here, nearly two hundred years later, Ronald Ames Guidry was born.

His father, Roland, working as a conductor for the Southern Pacific Railroad, was also a carpenter. As a small boy, Ron loved running. He ran from his house to the railroad yards in Lafayette to greet his homecoming father. In Roland's spare time, he and his small, dark son would spend hours in the peaceful Louisiana marshes duck hunting. Ron's love of running and a passion for football kept him too busy even to think about baseball. Every Christmas Ron asked for a football and every year one would be waiting for him under the Christmas tree. But one evening Ron ran from his house in tears because he had disobeyed his mother and she scolded him. The eight-year-old ran until he was stopped by a dead-end street. In a playground nearby the big kids, that is, the fourteen- and fifteen-year-olds, were playing a game of softball. They needed one more player to cover the outfield. Seeing Ron, they drafted him for the position. Although he was much younger than the

51

others, his speed and a strong, football-passing arm allowed Ron to keep up with the team. From that moment, his love of baseball was born.

He played every day in nearly every position: fielder, shortstop, first baseman, pitcher. Joining the Little League, Ron struck out teenagers who were five and six years older than he.

When he began high school, Ron played football and basketball, and also ran track for Northside School. And when the steamy Louisiana summers came, Ron lived and breathed baseball. He became a pitcher who did more than just fire a ball at the home plate. He used his mind along with the strength of his body to deliver winning pitches. He won a baseball scholarship to the University of Southwestern Louisiana in Lafayette. Ron soon heard that a semi-professional league in the Midwest needed players. Ron went to Liberal, Kansas, and although his nerves reduced him to the state of jelly, he still excelled during the tryouts for the team and was asked to join. While in Kansas, he began to develop the pitch that would turn him into a legend: the slider.

His pitches traveled at a speed that was usually only attained by men far larger and more muscular than this bony young Cajun. A scout for the New York Yankees baseball team spotted Ron's talent while he was playing in Kansas. On the recommendation of the scout, the Yankees drafted Ron to their club in 1971. He was sent to Johnson City, Tennessee. Before he could step into the hallowed arena that was Yankee Stadium, Bronx, New York, which had seen some of the most shimmering legends of the game—Babe Ruth, Lou Gehrig, Joe DiMaggio, Mickey Mantle— Ron had to work his way up from the minor leagues.

But when Ron joined the Yankees, the team was in a considerable slump. They hadn't won a World Series in over ten years. In 1973, George Steinbrenner bought the team from CBS Television and began recruiting the finest players he could find, offering some of them salaries that reached well into the millions of dollars.

In 1972, Ron married Bonnie Rutledge, his high school sweetheart. Four years later, he was playing in the Syracuse branch of the Yankees minor leagues and still had not been called up to New York for a permanent pitching job. On an evening in 1976, Ron and Bonnie began driving back to Louisiana. He was giving up. He planned to put aside all pitching dreams, face reality, and return to the quiet Louisiana marshes that were home to him. He planned to sit patiently in the duck blind, or play chess, and find some other type of employment to support his family.

They drove in silence for a long time. And then Bonnie, who at that moment probably knew her husband better than he knew himself, asked Ron if he was sure he wanted to give up baseball. A few miles later Ron admitted he wanted to give baseball one more try. He turned the car around and headed back to Syracuse. The young couple had no way of knowing that Bobby Cox, the manager of the Syracuse team, had just been told by the Yankee front office to work Ron as much as possible because they didn't plan to keep him in Syracuse for long.

On August 6, 1976, Ron was finally called to the majors. Sitting on the bench in the team dugout, amid splats of tobacco juice, Ron watched the other players. Under the guidance of first-string pitcher Sparky Lyle, he perfected his slider pitch. He played only sixteen innings, but he struck out twelve men at bat. Manager Billy Martin took sudden interest in the young Louisianian.

Then came 1977, and Ron had twenty-four straight

starts as a major league pitcher. His pitching was exceptional, and it helped bring the Yankees to the World Series to play against Tommy LaSorda's Los Angeles Dodgers.

It was a Saturday afternoon in October and a crucial game was about to be played. The Yankees needed to win if the tide of the series was going to be turned in their favor. The sky overhead was dazzling blue, and birds flew over Yankee Stadium like omens of good tidings. While the vendors hawked peanuts and popcorn, and the playing field gave off an aroma of newly mown grass, Ron stepped on the pitching mound. Going into the windup, one knee to his chest, he hurled the ball and struck like summer lightning in a bayou country sky. The Yankees won the game and went on to capture the World Championship. Ron was given the nickname "Louisiana Lightning."

The year 1978 would see the Dodgers and Yankees meeting again in another World Series. Once again, the Yankees won. By the end of the 1978 season Ron had become a world champion once more. That same year, he was the unanimous choice for the Cy Young pitching award, and he broke Babe Ruth's record of shutouts by a left-handed pitcher that had stood since 1916. The Yankees won thirty of the thirty-five games Ron started, and in one game against California he struck out eighteen men. The *Sporting News* named him Man of the Year. The Associated Press named him Male Athlete of the Year, and he was the *Baseball Quarterly's* Performer of the Year. In one season, he had established the major league record for the highest percentage of wins.

Until he retired from baseball in 1989, Ron remained with the Yankees. His fame and stunning success never went to his head. Working under an owner who had an explosive temper, Ron always remained calm. When he retired, the press wrote of him as an athlete who was also a gentleman, a class act who embodied the meaning of "sportsman."

In addition to baseball, Ron devoted many hours to the Special Olympics and served as the 1983 chairman. He described his efforts to serve humanity as the greatest work he ever did in his life. A six-year veteran of the National Guard, Ron is also an accomplished drummer.

There on the Eastern seaboard, not so very far from where his Cajun ancestors were expelled from Canada, Ron pitched his way into glory. The name "Louisiana Lightnin'" joined the ranks of other Yankee legends.

Ron, Bonnie, and their young family returned to Lafayette where they still live. His behavior on and off the field is a glowing testament of pride to the heritage of his native state.

MARGARET HAUGHERY

ON A FATEFUL DAY in 1818, William and Margaret Gaffney knelt before a priest to receive God's blessing and ask His protection. With three of their children, one of whom was a five-year-old girl also named Margaret, William and his wife were leaving Ireland. They were setting sail for America to escape the English grip that they believed was choking Ireland. Little Margaret's father was a tenant farmer who was tired of seeing the bigger part of his labors going to England while he and his family lived on the remaining tiny income. In addition to taking most of Ireland's income, the English considered the Irish an inferior race and never failed to let them know it.

Margaret's father had enough of it. Her mother had been an O'Rourke, and her O'Rourke ancestor, the Prince of Breffny, had been one of the most powerful Celtic chieftains. The Celts, an ancient race, had lived in Ireland, Scotland, and parts of France since Roman times. Little Margaret left the cool, Northern jewel of an island that was her home for Baltimore, never again to hear about banshees or leprechauns, nor imagine the strange cry of witches in the fog as she sat by the peat fire with her family at night. She would never see the cloudscapes in the Irish sky that, legend said, if you looked hard enough, would magically show you scenes from ages past.

In 1822, like an evil army of slithering ghosts, a yellow fever epidemic struck the city of Baltimore. Margaret's parents both died, and the little girl was now a homeless orphan. To this day, the fate of her brother is unknown. Her sister had died a few years earlier.

A woman named Mrs. Richards took the nine-year-old child into her home. Although not abused, Margaret worked as a servant to the Richards' for many years. Mrs. Richards, a Baptist by religion, one day prevented her from going to Mass when Margaret was a young woman. With trust in her God that would cause her to take risks throughout her life, she left Mrs. Richards and went out into the world with no-where to go. She found friends with whom she could worship according to her beliefs. One of these friends was Charles Haughery, the man she would love and then marry on October 10, 1835.

Charles Haughery was not of strong health, and the harsh Maryland winters were not kind to him. Margaret set sail from the confetti-colored fall land-scape of Maryland with her husband to arrive in the semi-tropical Crescent City. It was November 1835. Margaret and Charles felt at home in Catholic New Orleans. Despite Charles' frail health, the couple was very happy. In time a baby girl was born to them. Margaret was a joyous new wife and mother.

But doctors were unable to help Charles find a complete cure for his sickness and suggested that he go abroad. Charles Haughery wished to return to the tender green of Ireland and feel its soft cool mist stroke his face. Since there was not enough money for passage for the three of them, he left Margaret be-hind, waiting for weeks for some news from him. And then, she received word: he had died shortly after reaching Ireland.

Margaret Gaffney Haughery was twenty-three years old when she was widowed, left with only her child. And not so very long after the death of Charles, their little daughter became ill and also died. For a second time in her life, Margaret lost her entire family, and once more, she was alone.

Now without income, Margaret had to work in the laundry of the St. Charles Hotel. Daily, the Sisters of Charity passed the hotel, a group of thin, ragged orphans in tow. The orphanage was in obvious need of money, and the children's poverty seemed unfair to Margaret. Perhaps it was a longing to bundle her own little girl in protective layers against all harmful elements that made Margaret immediately resign her position at the laundry. Perhaps it was a realization that she could live out the spirit of her love for her daughter by giving love to other children that brought her to the steps of the Poydras Orphan Asylum the following morning. Seeking Sister Regis, the directress, she offered her services for a position there at less pay than her wages at the laundry. The sisters warmly welcomed her to the asylum.

In her early twenties, Margaret was a very pretty young woman who dressed neatly and plainly. A prim Quakeress' bonnet was always perched on her head whenever she went out. Since the nuns considered her to be of proper appearance and well mannered, one of her duties was to ask for donations from local merchants so the children could be clothed and fed. It was not beneath Margaret's dignity to push wheelbarrows of donated food throughout the streets of New Orleans, Quakeress bonnet, long skirts and all, to bring back to the hungry children.

The sisters gave Margaret free reign in her undertakings. The idea of failure only made her work harder to make certain that dreaded state never arrived, especially when it came to the betterment of life for the orphans.

By the end of 1836, the sisters had a dream of their own, and shared it with Margaret. The nuns wished to

59

withdraw from the Poydras Orphan Asylum and establish their own independent institution. They needed a house large enough, yet inexpensive enough so their small amount of money would not be gobbled up. It seemed hopeless, but then Margaret found "Old Withers" on New Levee Street.

It was the house's reputation for being haunted that made the rent so cheap. By day, it stood amid old, rotting trees draped with moss as grizzled and grey as the hair of a wizard. Dilapidated, with leaking roof, creaking doors that screeched when opened, and cobwebs that hung from the ceiling like winding sheets, the house was so dismal that the people of New Orleans were afraid to pass it even in daylight. At night, "Old Withers" was said to be "peopled" with specters who, shrouded and horned, shrieked and moaned, the sockets in their heads devoid of eyes and filled instead with internal fire.

Into this house of demons moved the nuns, Margaret, and their young charges.

And Margaret persevered. In time she was made manager of the orphanage. Soon the house was completely repaired, the children well fed and properly clothed, and New Orleans was astonished that the Catholic Orphan Asylum was peacefully coexisting with "ghosts."

But the children were not getting enough milk in their diet, and this worried Margaret. Using money she had saved from her days at the laundry, she bought dairy cows. The cows produced more milk than the children could drink, so Margaret sold the extra milk and gave the money to the orphanage. The demand for milk increased, and Margaret bought still more cows. She began to make delicious cream and butter and delivered these to her customers on a pushcart. Her business boomed. By 1840, Margaret's

60

profits from the dairy, along with some contributions of money from the community, enabled her to build St. Theresa's Orphan Asylum on Camp Street.

The yellow fever epidemics of the 1850s left thousands of New Orleans' children parentless. Thanks to Margaret, soon work began on the St. Vincent's Infant Asylum. A branch of the home, St. Elizabeth's House of Industry, was also founded in the 1850s by Margaret, and was a home for young ladies from ages twelve to eighteen. In addition, Margaret founded the Louise Home on Clio Street. To support the founding of these institutions, Margaret pushed her milk cart longer and farther throughout the city, for she provided the only source of funding for these undertakings.

And then, not long before the beginning of the Civil War, Margaret found herself the owner of a bakery by buying it from a bankrupt family as a favor. Thus, "Margaret's Bakery" was established.

Producing crusty breads, crispy soda crackers, cakes that were like puffs of clouds, delicious crumbly cookies, rich melt-away candy, *and* all kinds of pasta, the bakery was a success. With the combined income of bakery and dairy totaling over thirty thousand dollars annually, Margaret became an unlikely tycoon. The money raised went to the support of her charitable institutions and was also spread to the needy throughout the city. She had one "good" dress to her name, for use on Sundays and special occasions. She still saw her orphans daily. Her humility and simplicity never left her, nor did she abandon the grand adventure of living steeped in the faith she had for her God.

In 1862, at the time of New Orleans' fall to Yankee troops during the War Between the States, Margaret's two businesses were thriving. She carried basketloads of food to hungry households whose fathers had been killed in the war or were away fighting. She likewise gave relief to starving black people and runaway slaves. And carrying food to the poor nearly cost her very life.

The Union general in command of New Orleans was Benjamin Franklin "Beast" Butler. In addition to other acts of tyrannical brilliance, he had established picket lines in the city that were not to be crossed by anyone, on pain of death.

Margaret happily crossed these forbidden lines routinely to reach the poorest families who needed her food baskets. When General Butler made it known that he intended to hang Margaret Gaffney Haughery if she did not stop defying him, she paid him a visit. Telling him that she would continue to cross the picket lines until he hanged her, she then asked if he really believed Mr. Lincoln wanted to starve "helpless people to death." From that point, she then questioned General Butler about his reverence for life and God. When she had finished, Margaret came from the interview with a passport from the general that would ensure her safe conduct through the picket lines. As she continued to carry bread, milk, and flour to hungry people, she gained a reputation with the Union soldiers as "the only person of whom General Butler is afraid."

Margaret continued her work for another twenty years until illness took her from her beloved poor and placed her in a hospital. In February 1882, at the age of sixty-nine, Margaret died. Not long after her death, citizens who greatly missed the sight of her Quakeress' bonnet on her daily rounds, built the first statue in the United States ever to honor a woman. It is the likeness of a grandmotherly looking woman gazing down at a child in the crook of her arm. An inscription at the base of the statue simply reads "Margaret."

"Margaret" is a name derived from the Greek word *Margaron* which means "pearl." Irish legend tells us that a pot of gold can be found at the rainbow's end. Margaret Haughery was indeed a pearl for the city of New Orleans, and the love that was shown in her many acts of charity was both the rainbow's colors and legendary gold at its end. She fought the tyranny of poverty, hunger, and pestilence that can rob people of their hope, dignity, and life itself. She herself would not be tyrannized by inertia, self-pity, or grief. Perhaps the love Margaret would have poured out to her husband and child had they lived was given instead to an entire city. She left a legacy of caring in Louisiana that continued well into the twentieth century.

Sometimes the greatest of leaders are first the most obedient of servants.

LAFCADIO HEARN

PATRICK LAFCADIO HEARN was, by all accounts, a child of the sea. Born in 1850 on the Greek island Leucadia, for which he was named, the blue of the Mediterranean Sea and the sky above it were wondrously alive to him. The warmth of the Greek sun, the dark eyes of his mother bending over him, and the sound of sparkling blue water were memories he carried with him always. His mother brought him to Dublin, Ireland, to live with his Anglo-Irish father's family. She left him there following the breakup of her marriage. He was always lonely for the sight and smell of the sea and salt water. And for his mother.

His father, a soldier, also left Lafcadio and went to India. Lafcadio was raised by his elderly Aunt Sarah Brenane in a household steeped in strict tradition. When he first arrived in Ireland at the age of two, he was a nervous child with black hair hanging to his shoulders, one pierced ear, and enormous dark eyes. Aunt Sarah began turning what she considered a wild gypsy into a proper son of Irish gentry.

Locked in a dark bedroom by his aunt who believed this was the way to cure him of his fear of the dark, the child screamed night after night as he was "visited" by the demons of his imagination. His one source of comfort was a picture in the corner that showed a dark-eyed Madonna cradling her dark child. Little Lafcadio believed the lady was his mother and that he was the child she so lovingly held.

As he grew older the hurt he suffered because of his parent's separation began to heal somewhat as he spent happy summers away from his aunt at a family home on the South Irish coast. He loved to swim in the sea which had always been a friend to him. When he returned to Dublin, his time spent in the gloom and doom of Aunt Sarah's house bored him terribly. And then, one day, Lafcadio discovered the dusty, little-used library. Reading laid the fascinating world at his feet. His vivid imagination and restlessness escaped and soared into a world of words. Peacefully unsupervised, he spent hours with books as he would have with friends. He became acquainted with the people they were written about. Without taking a step from the dusty library, he traveled miles and miles through countries he never dreamed existed. The more he learned about the world, the more he discovered about himself. Reading Greek mythology one day, Lafcadio realized that he had a Greek love of beauty and knowledge. When his teen years arrived, Lafcadio was no longer tortured and lonely, but mischievous and unpredictable.

He was sent away to a school in Rouen, France, named *Institution Ecclésiastique.* Lafcadio hated the place. From this school, he next went to St. Cuthbert's in England. He was a practical joker, so good-natured and comical in his tricks that his professors laughed at him even as they punished him.

When he was sixteen and playing a school game called "Giant's Stride," Lafcadio was accidentally struck in the left eye by a piece of knotted rope. Surgery was performed, but the sight in his eye was permanently lost. Moreover, scar tissue from the operation grew and covered one of the teenager's extraordinary eyes with a white layer. Believing himself to be hideously deformed, Lafcadio was no longer the fun-loving trickster of St. Cuthbert's.

By 1869, Aunt Sarah, growing older and more feeble, was nearly penniless. Lafcadio had to be withdrawn from school. A nephew who had gotten into Aunt Sarah's good graces, not to mention her pocketbook, told Lafcadio that he eventually would be sent to America to live with another branch of the family in Ohio. Nearly nineteen years old, Lafcadio arrived in Cincinnati only to discover that the relative he looked for was in no financial condition to support him. Frightened, alone, frequently starving, he often slept in alleyways.

One day a man named Henry Watkins, the owner of a print shop, met Lafcadio. The young immigrant ran errands, tidied papers, and swept paper shavings from the floor for Mr. Watkins in exchange for food, a warm bed, and fatherly advice. At last Lafcadio had found a friend.

Lafcadio began to find jobs on small newspapers. In 1872, he showed the managing editor of the *Cincinnati Enquirer* a sample of his writing. The piece was accepted for publication. More writing assignments were given to the slight twenty-three-year-old writer. For ten years, he walked the gaslit streets of Cincinnati observing its night life, reporting on gruesome murders, levee camps, criminals, and the odd characters found in a river town. He once even dressed as a woman to obtain a story. In 1877, he was given an assignment to travel to New Orleans and live there for a while as he reported on Louisiana politics.

He fell in love with exotic sun-washed New Orleans and its hodgepodge of cultures. He loved the city's closeness to the waters that, rushing and swirling, surrounded it, giving it life. New Orleans could be as glaring white and bright as Greece and as rainy and grey-skied as Ireland.

Lafcadio resigned from the Cincinnati job and became assistant editor of the newly founded *New Or-*

leans Item. The newspaper published stories of police corruption and crooked dealings.

His translations for the *Item* of the works of French writers made Lafcadio famous throughout America. Lafcadio's own writing style was developing. His stories of New Orleans Creoles, black people, Louisiana folklore, Mardi Gras, and the scariness of voodoo began appearing in *Harper's Weekly,* a Northern magazine. He collected recipes for a book called, *La Cuisine Creole.*

It was on one of his trips to Grand Isle, among the oak and citrus trees twisted by Gulf winds in South Jefferson Parish that the idea for a novelette came into his mind. In the middle of the nineteenth century, a hurricane struck a resort named *L'Ile Dernière,* which is French for "Last Island." While the storm blew, hundreds of people on the island were drowned and swept into the Gulf by a tidal wave as they supposedly danced to waltz music played at a foolhardy hurricane ball. From Lafcadio's pen came *Chita,* based on the true story of a Creole infant pulled from the sea alive, clasped in her dead mother's arms after the hurricane. *Harper's Weekly* gladly accepted the novelette for printing. Lafcadio gave up his job as a reporter and turned to freelance writing full time.

He left New Orleans and wrote for two years on the island of Martinique in the Caribbean, once a stopping point for pirates. He then lived briefly in New York. At the suggestion of *Harper's Weekly,* Lafcadio went to Japan. Very little was known about the Far East in America. Lafcadio was supposed to live one year in Japan, and then write about that mysterious country. He left New York in March 1890 on a train that carried him across the entire snowy span of Canada to icy Alaska. From Alaska he sailed across the Pacific Ocean and awakened one April dawn to see the peak of Mount Fuji above Tokyo looking like an icicle lit by the rising sun.

Just as when he first saw New Orleans, he immediately fell in love with Japan. He studied its music, customs, and its religion, Buddhism. He completed his writing assignment for *Harper's* and decided to stay. In Japan, the always struggling Lafcadio at last found peace and security.

Becoming an English tutor at a school in a rural town, he soon married a daughter of a proud family. Her name was Setsu, a Japanese word meaning "true."

He explored the islands of Japan, its mountains and seascapes. He listened to its strange tales and superstitions. He wrote *Kwaidan,* or "ghost stories," which is a collection of tales based on Japanese legends. Four of the stories were used in a movie of the same name, filmed nearly one hundred years after Lafcadio wrote them.

The Imperial University of Japan in Tokyo offered him the position of professor of English literature. His books were published year after year: *Out of the East, Glimpses of an Unfamiliar Japan,* and *Japan: An Attempt at Interpretation.*

Lafcadio's and Setsu's family soon included four children. He devoted himself first to them. He was determined that his children would never suffer the kind of childhood and youth he had endured. They were a very happy family. Each evening at sunset, Lafcadio and his children would stand overlooking Tokyo Bay and sing the words to a song that would be inscribed on a memorial to him after his death: "Evening burning! Little burning! Weather be fair tomorrow!"

In September 1904, Lafcadio died, his wife at his side.

Whether he was capturing the spice and pepper of New Orleans, or the opal-like quality of Japan, his writings were like color washes on silk screens. His work gave lasting testimony to whatever culture it represented at the time, and sparkled like crystal drops of water from the blue glass of his beloved sea.

CLEMENTINE HUNTER

PRIMARY COLORS. Red, yellow, and blue, the three from which all others are born. Blue, crimson, yellow, green, ivory, and black. Tubes of oil squeezed, a brush dipped into the jewels of jellied color on a makeshift palette and guided along anything available—a canvas, a window shade, a paper bag, a plywood board—by her hands trying to capture the image she sees in her mind.

Mix colors, Clementine. Red and blue will give you purple eggplants, red and yellow will give you orange zinnias, and blue and yellow will give you the green of the trees and fields in which you once picked cotton and gathered pecans. On your canvas, paint the rose of that tiny skirt drying on the clothesline so that it matches the rose-colored streak of the sunset in the blue popsicle color of your sky.

Paint, Clementine, while the smell of turpentine and linseed oil makes your head dizzy. Outside the chickens will scratch and peck in the yard, and not far away the silver fish will jump in the Cane River flowing past the wrought-iron confectionery of the balconies of Natchitoches.

She was christened Clementine, daughter of Antoinette Adams and Janvier Reuben. She was born in the mid-winter of either 1886 or 1887, on a cotton plantation named Hidden Hill near Cloutierville. Her father, she claimed, was French, her grandfather Irish, and her grandmother, MeMe, was a black woman who was also part Indian.

Her family, always needing an extra set of hands to help with the unending work, never forced Clementine to continue her education. By the time she was in her early teens, she was a swift and nimble field worker.

In 1769, an enterprising slave woman named Marie Thérèse CoinCoin, who had acquired her own freedom and that of her children, also acquired a plantation near the Cane River.

In 1898, the vacant house and ruined grounds were purchased by John Henry Hampton and his wife, "Cammie." Cammie's ambition was to restore the plantation she now christened Melrose to the days of Marie Thérèse CoinCoin's glorious possession. The grounds, main house, and outbuildings were repaired and renovated. Hoping to turn Melrose into a center for the preservation of Louisiana history, culture, and handicraft, Cammie became friends with artists and writers. As Cammie's guests, they flocked to the serenity and beauty of Melrose much like the religious who flock to monasteries and cloisters for peace and adoration.

Clementine came to Melrose Plantation at some point in her life between childhood and young womanhood, still an industrious little worker in the fields picking cotton. When the air turned crisp and crystallike in the autumn, Clementine gathered bushels of pecans season after season.

When she was in her thirty-ninth year, Clementine married Emmanuel Hunter and together they raised five children. Cammie Henry soon took Clementine out of the fields, and she became a maid on the house staff. She began to show her talent for creative cookery, inventing dishes which were enjoyed by the famous guests at the Henry table. Clementine listened to many discussions about books and art as she moved about the houseguests serving after-dinner coffee, or pecan pie, or Cane River fish delicately cooked to savor. She was also talented with her handicraft. She wove baskets and spun lace as delicate and intricate as a spider's gossamer web. The quilts she made were of her own design, bright splashes of color to awaken the drabbest of rooms. Her high-cheekboned face, bandanna-covered head, and manner which was both lively and dignified at the same time affectionately became part and parcel of Melrose Plantation.

By the 1930s, Cammie Henry's Melrose consisted of a plantation library and museum collections of history. It was in need of a person to be responsible for its books, papers, and grounds. Cammie offered the position to her friend François Mignon. He was a Frenchman and talented writer. He arrived at Melrose in 1938 to take up permanent residence.

One morning in 1940, Clementine knocked at his door. In her hand she clutched tubes of paint cast off by an artist who had been painting in the room Clementine had been told to clean. To Monsieur Mignon that morning, Clementine expressed a desire to paint. He found some old paint brushes along with an old windowshade. Clementine accepted them and a few hours later returned to his room with her finished first picture. He was amazed at what he saw. He became her mentor; she became addicted to painting. Unable to afford art supplies, she scrounged for the half-empty tubes of paint left by Cammie Henry's guests. Occasionally she received a surprise gift of paints ordered from Sears and Roebuck by François Mignon.

Working the entire day at the big house, taking laundry home at night, caring for a sick husband, it was usually past midnight when Clementine could sit down to paint. Cardboard boxes, empty bottles, paper bags, all were painted in the light of an oil lamp and turned into scenes of vivid life by hands just about to enter their sixth decade.

Clementine's career was further encouraged by the arrival of an Oklahoma writer named James Register. Like Mignon, he fell in love with her childlike paintings. After leaving Melrose, he regularly sent art supplies, paints, brushes, and paper from Oklahoma. He obtained for her the Julius Rosenwald Foundation Grant that would help fund her artistic work.

Messrs. Mignon and Register had other plans, and exposed her works to critics and the public. By 1945, she had small showings of her paintings in galleries in Texas.

Then came 1949 and the New Orleans Art and Craft Show. Her works were featured, and critics praised her as a true primitive painter. Fellow artists declared that her art was the best of all works presented in that particular show.

In 1953, the June issue of *Look,* a magazine that was as popular at the time as *People* or *Time* magazine today, named Clementine one of the best American primitive artists.

Clementine's fame spread to the new medium of television. She was to be called the "Black Grandma Moses."

Through the three decades that would follow, her paintings were an unending supply of treasures for art lovers around the world. She had sold her first paintings for twenty-five cents in the 1940s; the 1980s would see each of her works sell for thousands of dollars. Her nine rooms of painted walls in the African House at Melrose would help place the plantation on the National Register of Historic Places in 1972. She was included in many books on the folk painters of America. Magazine stories were frequently written about her.

In 1976, one of her paintings was part of the United Nations' UNICEF calendar. In 1984, her paintings were shown in art galleries of both New York and Washington, D.C. Northwestern State University gave her the honorary degree of Doctor of Fine Arts in 1986.

She belonged to the school of primitive artists, those gifted beings who come by their ability naturally, without ever studying art. The themes of their paintings are borrowed from everyday life as they know it. In Clementine's instance, it was revival meetings in churches and baptisms in the Cane River, Saturday nights at the honky-tonk, or washing clothes in a big black pot. Like the prehistoric people who left their drawings on stony cave walls, and the Indians who followed them, the same instinct to show life in pictures was in Clementine. Her paintings were like a celebration, a jubilee, the colors and figures as happy and different as a box of crayons.

On January 1, 1988, Clementine Hunter died. She had just begun the second century of her life. But the life she had lived, its memories along with the impressions of her mind, were spread across her many canvasses in paintings. And always, that joyous color.

GRACE KING

. . . prisms

IT WAS APRIL 1862. The War Between the States had journeyed through twelve months to reach its first birthday. The candles on its cake were barrels of cannons and bayonets glowing from musket fire; its icing deep red. And at this first birthday, the city of New Orleans was sliced and served, conquered and presented to Mr. Lincoln.

A few days before the fall of New Orleans, Grace Elizabeth King, nearly ten years old, watched from the third-floor window of her Camp Street home as the cotton bales and other Confederate army supplies were set afire by retreating Southern soldiers. The levee of the Mississippi was lined with bonfires scorching the night sky. Alarm bells sounded simultaneously with explosions. And not long after New Orleans fell, Union soldiers burst into Grace's home seeking her father, William Woodson King, a successful attorney, for questioning. They were met with cool dignity by Grace's mother, Sarah, a lady descended from Alsatian Huguenots and Scotch Presbyterians, and Grace's equally haughty grandmother, Eliza. Unknown to the soldiers, two of William King's little sons were scuttling through the streets of New Orleans with a warning to him from their mother that he was in trouble. He slipped away from the city that night, sending word to his wife that she and their children were to join him as soon as possible at their secluded plantation named L'Embarrass in Iberville Parish.

Bayou L'Embarrass was a destination Grace's mother had only a vague idea of how to reach. Above all, facing her was the difficult task of obtaining a

79

passport for the entire family from Union Gen. Benjamin Butler, a commander well known for hostility against New Orleanians, especially women. The pass was denied. Mrs. King met with another general by chance as she was leaving Union headquarters and the general obtained for her the pass Butler had refused.

On a night in October, the remainder of the King household left the gracious home where they had lived in antebellum affluence. As Grace was lifting her pantalette-covered little leg to climb into the carriage, a mysterious person pushed a battered rag doll into her arms. She later discovered that the doll was filled with Confederate money to be sent to a soldier in Northern Louisiana. The carriages took them to the banks of the river where they boarded a Federal steamer on the night-blackened Mississippi River. They came under fire from the rifles of the Confederate guerrillas. The seven King children were terrified, but their grandmother gathered them together protectingly and no one was hurt. The following morning found them leaving the steamboat looking for L'Embarrass in a downpour. Night after night the family asked for food and shelter at plantations that dotted the riverside. The family once even crossed a body of water on a ferry that was half-burned. Boarding still another steamboat that was also carrying Confederate soldiers, Grace's mother told the rebels stories about the Yankee soldiers in New Orleans. Later that night, now traveling by rowboat and having run aground on a bayou, they were lost. But the family heard a familiar voice calling to them out of the black stillness of the night. The Confederate soldiers his family had traveled with earlier in the day had met with Mr. King by chance. They told him about a New Orleans lady with seven children in tow who was

80

looking for L'Embarrass. Deciding that the lady could only be his wife, he set out to find her, and he and his family were reunited at last.

Far away from the city and schools, their parents continued to see that their children were educated. They were encouraged to read Shakespeare and the English Romantic poets, and to study the speeches of Revolutionary War orators such as Patrick Henry. Grace, a dark-eyed little girl whose hair hung in natural ringlets, loved words. One winter night, as the cannon fire of the Civil War boomed in the distance, Grace's brother read tales of Scotland aloud. As she sat with her brothers and sisters in the orange light of a hearth fire, her imagination carried her to the peaceful violet and green mountains of the Scottish highlands. One morning, in a blaze of sunlight on the edge of the cypress forest near her home, Grace solemnly vowed to the green mirror of the bayou, and its creatures, that one day she would be a writer.

The homespun plantation life at L'Embarrass exposed Grace to the handicrafts of candlemaking, spinning, sewing, and weaving carried out by skilled black hands. With her brothers and sisters, she learned about farm animals, planting, and harvest. Her father was kind to the slaves; in turn, he was respected by them and had their affection.

When Confederate general Robert E. Lee surrendered at Appomattox in Virginia and Grace returned to New Orleans with her family, her father was ruined financially. Humiliated by poverty, the family had to live in a cramped house. Yet Grace's education continued despite her family's hardships. She excelled in her studies, particularly French, which, true to the quarter portion of her blood that was Alsatian, she spoke with the fluency of a New Orleans Creole. Beginning to build in Grace was a yearning for independence, a desire to earn her own way and somehow restore her family's lost pride.

An argument would be the catalyst to set Grace King's destiny in motion.

One of the Crescent City's native sons, George Washington Cable, had written a series of fictional works on prominent Creoles in antebellum New Orleans, which said that they were cruel slave owners who enjoyed torturing their servants. Grace had been a friend of many a fine Creole family and knew that Cable's stories were untrue exaggerations. Cruelty to slaves was an exception to the everyday life of antebellum New Orleans' Creole society.

Cable's publisher, a Northern gentleman named Richard Watson Gilder, came to New Orleans in 1885. Meeting by chance at the Pickwick Club, Mr. Gilder expressed shock to Grace that New Orleans was so hostile towards Mr. Cable. Grace told him she felt that Cable had stabbed New Orleans in the back with his stories. Mr. Gilder replied with an insult that would change her life forever: If Cable was so dishonest in his writings of New Orleans, why had no New Orleanian published any better writings of his own?

Inwardly seething, Grace bade Cable a stiff good night.

The next morning, Grace Elizabeth, still fuming, sat at her writing table in her room, picked up her pen and wrote her first story *Monsieur Motte*. Its heroine is Marcelite, a quadroon hairdresser loved by the Creole family she serves. Marcelite secretly and unselfishly aids the family's daughter whom she loves as a sister.

Monsieur Motte was published in the *New Princeton Review* in 1886. Grace was thirty-three years old. The story was well received, and more of her work was requested. By May of 1887, when the prestigious Northern-based *Harpers Magazine* included her in a series of sketches called "The Recent Movement in Southern Literature," Grace had definitely arrived. She had gained a reputation as a valid literary representative of Southern life. She became close friends with Samuel Langhorne Clemens, more commonly known as Mark Twain. He admired her work tremendously, as did the masterful writer Henry James.

With her works, *Tales of a Time and Place, Balcony Stories, A History of New Orleans, The Pleasant Ways of St. Medard*, Grace had achieved her dream of independence and the restored pride of the name of King. She had also given a measure of vindication to the conquered South. In the course of her life, she traveled to France to research Jean-Baptiste Le Moyne, Sieur de Bienville, and Hernando de Soto. Her book, *La Dame de Sainte Hermine*, told the story of the early settlement of Louisiana. In 1892, she lectured on American writer Sydney Lanier at Newham College in Cambridge, England.

The same week in November of 1918 that saw the end of World War I also saw Grace honored by France, a country that decorated her with the gold palms of *Officier de l'Instruction Publique*. In the final year of her life, she penned her memoirs.

In 1932, at the age of eighty, Grace died at her home on Coliseum Street.

What started as an insulted Southerner answering a challenge developed into a regional writer who was praised around the world. Her writings captured for the world a New Orleans that is forever lost to us, except through the pages of her books. She was a very proud woman who had seen her beloved homeland humiliated by Confederate defeat and Reconstruction, and insulted by one of its own sons in the presses of the victorious North. But she fought back with her pen, her mind, and the strongest of weapons, truth.

In her later years, the house on Coliseum Street that she shared with her two sisters was filled with prisms, those sometimes musical creations that cut light down to show the hidden colors that live within it. She was like a prism in her writings, and the color that was New Orleans in the nineteenth century filtered through her own mind and presented itself to the world by way of her pen.

The clarity of her vision was a fitting looking glass.

HUEY P. LONG

HUEY PIERCE LONG was born in Winnfield, Louisiana, on August 30, 1893. His bloodlines were a combination of Dutch, French, Scottish, Welsh, and Irish ancestry. Yet in his way, he was classically American: pushy, determined, revolutionary. Of the ten children born to his father, Huey, and his mother, Caledonia, he was the eighth. His great grandfather, James, a Methodist minister born in Maryland, was descended from the Long family that had been in America since well before the time of the American Revolution.

Huey's performance in his school work at Winnfield High School won him a scholarship to Louisiana State University. Despite his scholarship, he still had financial problems. He sold pie plates and cookbooks door-to-door, attended school in Oklahoma and Shreveport, and finally in New Orleans at Tulane University. In 1913, he married Rose McConnell and eventually became the father of three children. When Huey was twenty-one, he passed a bar examination and began his law practice back in his hometown of Winnfield.

Since he had been a young boy, the political rallies of Winnfield had fascinated him. In 1918, the people of the North Louisiana District elected Huey railroad commissioner. Upon his re-election to the commission in 1921, he became its chairman. There was no job or request for improvement that Huey overlooked as railroad commissioner: a cistern needed by tiny Bordelonville, or the raising of a platform in other hamlets—Huey listened to each person's complaint and forced railroad companies to correct any problem.

He was beginning to win the undying gratitude of the poor people in Louisiana, and the poor in the state at that time were in vast numbers.

In 1924, Huey entered the governor's race and lost. He ran once more in 1928, won the election and ruled Louisiana like a king, thus receiving the nickname, "Kingfish." In 1929, the nation's banks lost all of their money, and the country plunged into the era known as the Depression.

When the state legislature refused to pass bills he approved of, Huey would appear on the legislative floor to make sure that the bills were enacted in the next round of voting. He fought for, and won, a free textbook law. He spent millions of state dollars to improve the horrid highway and bridge conditions of Louisiana. His tendency to bend the law, usually to help the poor people of the state, nearly got him thrown out of office in 1929. This was prevented by fifteen senators who voted against his removal.

In 1930, Huey was elected to the U.S. Senate and acted as both governor and senator-elect. Dark-haired, with a pug nose and wide smile, Huey clowned by signing legislative bills before photographers in hot-pink pajamas. When the poverty of the Depression had Louisianians by the throat, he promised them a share in wealth, proclaiming, "every man a king!" The majority of the desperate people believed him for he offered them hope. The state was becoming more modern. He was the governor of the little man, and as the little man's loyalty grew, so did Huey's power. Responsible for building the present-day state capitol building, he also made sure that Louisiana State University received funding that improved its standing as a major college, while starting the New Orleans branch of the LSU Medical School. In 1932, he helped O. K. Allen become governor of

Louisiana before he went to Washington as a United States senator. From Washington, Huey had laws instituted that ended local self-government in Louisiana, and allowed him to have complete control over the police and fire forces, the legal system, education, state militia, and officials who governed elections. He was the Kingfish, and Louisiana was his kingdom.

And he wished for a wider kingdom. The plans that had helped him gain such control over Louisiana were beginning to have the same effect in Washington. In 1932, he had supported Franklin Roosevelt for president. One year later, he turned against Roosevelt. The very liberal president considered Huey a radical because of his ideas for spreading the nation's wealth among the Depression-stricken poor. Huey's influence in Washington made his fame second only to President Roosevelt's throughout the nation. Huey's political speeches and gestures were explosive. Throughout the years, his style of speaking and its hold upon audiences would be compared to Adolph Hitler. Huey wrote the books *Every Man a King* and *My First Days in the White House.* He co-wrote and published music. He had conquered the slow and backwards, stick-in-the mud politicians of Louisiana and had dragged them into the twentieth century, and by God, he would do the same to the United States of America.

It was September 8, 1935, and a special session of the state legislature had been called. He had been both governor and senator of the great state of Louisiana and had just announced he'd also like to be president of these United States very soon. It was nine o'clock at night, and Huey was about to address the Louisiana House of Representatives. Although he had given up both alcohol and smoking for a long time, he had a sudden, unexplainable craving for the incense-like, vanilla-rich taste of a good cigar. He gave into the desire and told one of his supporters, young Jimmie O'Connor, to run to the restaurant in the basement of the state capitol building and bring him some cigars.

Twenty minutes later, he was striding down a corridor, headed for his office. A man in a white suit stepped from behind a pillar and walked towards him. The white-suited man, Dr. Carl Weiss, pointed a pistol at him and fired. Huey screamed, "I'm shot!" and reeled and lurched down the nearby basement stairs that Jimmie O'Connor was just climbing to bring him the cigars he'd been craving.

He was still conscious when Jimmie O'Connor helped a nurse and young doctor wheel him into an operating room at Our Lady of the Lake Hospital in Baton Rouge. He had been shot below the ribs and surgery was necessary or he'd bleed to death. With the operating room filled with politicians who streamed out into the hall, the doctors began surgery and, when they had finished, declared he would survive. But specialists from New Orleans who arrived later discovered that the surgeon had missed seeing damage to his kidneys. It was too dangerous to operate again. He grew weaker, and as he lay in his bed, it seemed he saw masses of poor people coming to him, begging him to help them, ragged people with pleading eyes, who needed him as their president. He was forty-two years old, he had his whole life ahead of him, there was so much he still had to do.

On September 10, 1935, Huey Pierce Long died. By a special act of the state legislature, he was buried at the base of the state capitol, the skyscraper he helped construct, a symbol of the new Louisiana he had helped to build.

JOHN McDONOGH

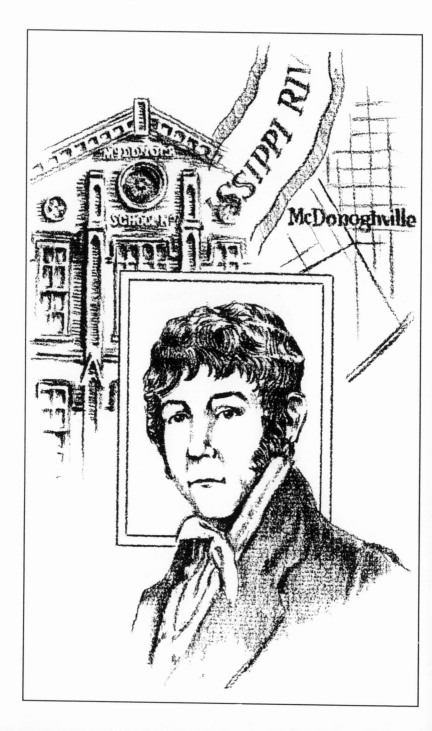

. . . the gifts of the steward

JOHN McDONOGH was born in Baltimore, Maryland, on December 29 when the nation was but three years old. His father was also named John, and hailed from York County, Pennsylvania. He had served under George Washington in the Revolutionary War. Elizabeth Wilkins McDonogh bore twelve children, the sixth of whom was John, the eldest son and named for his father. After the American army defeated the British, John Sr. resumed his business and land-owning practices. His children's upbringing consisted of being steeped in both religion and education. True to their Scotch-Irish blood, they were a close-knit family who gave of their love to one another through honest, caring deeds instead of flowery displays of affection.

When young John was nearly seventeen years old, his father placed him as a clerk in a merchant house owned by William Taylor. Mr. Taylor, well read as most book lovers are, traded with the West Indies, Europe, and the regions still under Spanish rule in America. He recognized in his young clerk traits of industry and courtesy, and an eye for detail. He was quiet but his disposition was pleasant and cheerful.

By 1800, Mr. Taylor trusted the boy so much that he sent him to New Orleans as his business representative. Dark-haired, dark-eyed, and rather baby-faced when he arrived in New Orleans, John was barely twenty years old. Two years later, Mr. Taylor suffered serious business difficulties, yet John remained loyal to him. By 1803, Mr. Taylor's drooping trade received a boost as a result of the Louisiana

Purchase and the prosperity it brought to American business. Mr. Taylor began to flourish once more and John began his own personal prospering. John started buying his own land and property and also built warehouses in New Orleans.

Living in a townhouse at the corner of Chartres and Toulouse streets described as splendid, John also acquired several plantations. In his boyhood, John's mother had been a loving example of both duty and devotion to her husband and children. John loved her very much and, as a result of his relationship with his mother, respected all women. As a young man in New Orleans, whose heart was softer than his quiet manner would seem to indicate, he fell in love with the daughter of Don Almonstre y Roxas. This New Orleans beauty who would later take her own place in New Orleans history as the Baroness Pontalba, was sought in marriage by John. She was Catholic, he was a Presbyterian, and their religious differences prevented their marriage. Three years later after his doomed courtship with the future Baroness, John's heart was captured once more by another New Orleans' beauty, known only as "Miss Johnson." Once again, John's religion prevented him from marrying a Catholic. Miss Johnson later entered a convent.

When John realized that marriage was a more difficult state for him to enter than it seemed to be for other men, he lapsed into serious soul searching. Like the pharaoh who had stored grain and food during the years of plenty to survive the years of famine, he reasoned, couldn't his wealth and the results of his labor be saved and stored during his life, then given to the needy after his death? He would be without his own wife and children but he could serve the family of man throughout generations if he worked hard enough during his lifetime. He was old-fashioned, even for his time, and the kinds of charms that meant the ruin of many young men held little appeal for this sturdy and practical Scotch-Irishman. Considered cold and distant in his dealings with others, John only desired the private satisfaction of knowing that he was doing what was right. Bent on his dreams of helping the needy, he became even quieter and worked harder than ever. The plan he mapped out for himself was stamped in his mind and carved in his spirit.

John spent the next ten years accumulating his fortune and helping to educate two of his younger brothers. And then, it was January 1815. John took his place on the green fields of Chalmette with the Americans and, like his father had before him, confronted the British. Belonging to Beale's Rifles, a crack volunteer New Orleans regiment, John helped maintain the American freedom of New Orleans.

That same year John decided to give up life in the city. He moved to one of his plantations on the West Bank of the Mississippi River, in a suburb that would later be known as "McDonoghville." He lived in a simple country house. He was in his mid-thirties and very wealthy. He was ready to turn all of his attention to his dream of giving to the poor. John lived simply, yet comfortably. In him was no desire to advertise his wealth by high living. He had not worked so hard during his early manhood to impress people because of his possessions; he had worked to be true to the principle that all should be done to "glorify God"— whether God felt sufficiently glorified by John is a matter between John and the Almighty.

In 1817, when his old employer William Taylor went bankrupt, John invited him to live in his own home where Mr. Taylor stayed the rest of his life.

In addition to Mr. Taylor, John took charge of caring for orphans, some of whom lived at his house or were sent to school by him. He could not stress enough the importance of an education for both boys and girls. Yet, true to the ideas of his time, he believed that girls should not possess more education than boys because, when they married, it would cause jealousy on the husband's part and great unhappiness in marriage for the wife. Young ladies were to be spared that concern.

Meanwhile, John was still attending the accounts of his business enterprises and purchasing property. Considering himself a "steward of the Lord," he purchased, by degrees, all the swamps, farms, tracts, lands, and acreage that were encircling the boundaries of the city of New Orleans. This made him one of the most extensive landowners of his time. In 1844, he anonymously helped establish a public school library and lyceum.

On the last day of his life in 1850, some New Orleans townspeople were aghast to see John McDonogh actually pay money, actually hand over some of his precious hoard of wealth, to ride a tram instead of relying on his usual way of traveling: walking. The people didn't realize that he took the tram because he felt too ill to walk, any more than they knew that he believed a man capable of walking ought to do so instead of, out of laziness, spending money that could be given to the poor. That day, all the citizens saw was the lanky old man in his clothes that were of a style belonging to the previous century, breaking his tight-fisted habits by boarding public transportation.

John died that night at his plantation. When the will he had made under such secrecy in 1838 was read, it revealed provisions for the founding of a shelter for the poor, and the Society for the Relief of Destitute Orphan Boys in New Orleans. He left money for the establishment of farm schools throughout his native Maryland. The remaining half of his fortune was to go to the part of life he felt most important to a man's dignity and survival: education. Dividing the rest of his fortune equally between New Orleans and Baltimore, his will stated that it was to be used to set up a network of free public schools for the poor. His legacy fostered the widespread birth of free public schools throughout the city of New Orleans.

John's stewardship on earth had been well planned, and the full measure of his giving was realized by a shamefaced city. But had he been alive, John would not have required their shame, nor asked any apology. He had hoarded in the name of God and had given in the same Name. Like the Magi on their journey, he had followed a star that only he could see inwardly. He carried with him the gifts that hard work had earned, and like those three wandering kings, he would not give his gifts away until the star showed him the journey's end.

Found among his personal effects after his death were a dainty lady's slipper and a silken sliver of a ribbon. It was said that they had belonged to Miss Johnson, who had become a nun. How John happened to obtain these, and under what circumstances, can only be imagined.

ELEANOR McMAIN

ELEANOR McMAIN was born on March 2, 1868, in a cottage near the banks of the Amite River. A few years before her birth, Eleanor's parents fled from their home in Baton Rouge to escape the Yankee army that was creeping up the Mississippi River from the Gulf of Mexico. She was born to a family already filled with brothers. As Eleanor grew, her genteel mother schooled her little daughter to be a lady, while her brothers included Eleanor in all of their games and adventures on the Amite River. As a result, Eleanor was a high-spirited tomboy in addition to being a polite and considerate child. She could almost angelically recite her Bible lessons, and then not so angelically give into the sheer delight of jumping on the feather mattresses in her home along with her siblings. Her home life was a happy one. Coming from so large a family taught Eleanor about sharing. Her parents instilled in her a strong sense of justice and honesty. When she became a young woman, Eleanor was quiet and well educated.

Often times, women who were tomboys in childhood seem blessed with extraordinary understanding and patience when it comes to young people and children. Eleanor, as an adult, was no exception to this rule. She became a teacher, and in time, joined the staff of Newcomb College in New Orleans.

From the 1870s and into the twentieth century, there were many movements in New Orleans to help the poor people of the city. The Irish, in particular, were forced to live in squalor. Having escaped Ireland's famine in the mid-nineteenth century to settle in America, the Irish worked at bone-breaking labor that frequently killed them, and for meager pay. They were harshly discriminated against for no other reason except that they were Irish. In a section of New Orleans still known as the Irish Channel, where tragedies were daily occurrences, the immigrants settled. But a kind-hearted group of people from Trinity Episcopal Church started a settlement house in the Irish Channel, working to give the neighborhood's people as much assistance as possible. It was 1901 and Eleanor was thirty-three years old. She was still teaching at Newcomb College when she heard about the wonderful things the settlement house was accomplishing.

Trinity Episcopal Church was planning to expand the services of the settlement house that would become known as Kingsley House to include a kindergarten. Although she needed to take additional courses at that time, Eleanor applied herself and joined Kingsley House. In a few years' time, she was made its leader.

Eleanor did more than just teach. She ventured out into the Irish Channel and visited the community. Using an overturned bucket for a seat, Eleanor would speak with women as they hung their wash out to dry in their yards. Always confronted with the needs and problems of the people she visited regularly, Eleanor would then see to it that the problem was solved: Food would be found for a hungry family's table, medical care for the ill or handicapped, and child care for a destitute family wherein both parents had to work.

In a community that had no drinking water except the rain that was collected in unsanitary cisterns, Eleanor opened the pump at Kingsley House so the entire neighborhood could have buckets of fresh water whenever they wanted. The many filthy gutters of the

Irish Channel, filled with dirty stagnant water, helped breed rampant mosquito populations. Mosquitos, carriers of the dreaded yellow fever, brought even more disease and death to the Irish community whenever summertime seared New Orleans. One day, Eleanor, her dark eyes glinting with determination, took a broom and shovel and began cleaning the gutters. She cleared away the standing water in the streets. Seeing their beloved and genteel Miss McMain performing street cleaning made the neighborhood follow her example. They kept the channel clear of dirty gutters and water. Eleanor had the gutters fumigated and disinfected regularly. Due largely to her initiative, whenever yellow fever struck in the city, few cases of the disease were reported in the Irish Channel.

Finding a shady house with wide, deep porches in the country, on the banks of Lake Pontchartrain, Eleanor began Camp Onward. It was a summer getaway for her young students. On the very first day Eleanor, her staff, and the children were enjoying a picnic at the camp, it began to rain. They ran to the porch to wait for the rain to end. Soon the wind began screaming, blowing the teeming rain in horizontal lines. It was the early twentieth century, there was no radar, nor radio communications, and thus, no way for anyone to know when or where a hurricane was about to hit. There by the lake, Eleanor and her students were trapped by an unpleasant surprise.

The water of the lake rose and came rushing through Camp Onward. Eleanor, with the help of her staff, fought through the swirling flood and enormous wall of high winds and got all of her children to higher ground and safety. No one was badly injured.

Eleanor also fought to abolish child labor laws. Her hard work to make others realize the needs of the poor helped establish New Orleans' first playground, a recreation system, and a tenement, or project, house code.

She journeyed to France on an invitation to establish an institution similar to Kingsley House in Paris. Her field work in what was the misery of the Irish Channel gave her the knowledge to found the Tulane University School of Social Work.

Kingsley House survives to this day, serving the African-American and Hispanic cultures who now live in the Irish Channel.

Eleanor was an example to nearly everyone whose life she touched. To some she was a role model of cleanliness or knowledge; to others, she was an example of unselfish caring that made people look past their own concerns and help those more in need.

Eleanor McMain died in 1934. At Claiborne and Nashville Avenues, a high school bearing her name attracts students from the entire city. Eleanor's real triumph was in each person she saved from oppression and poverty and in each individual she gently guided until he was at last strong enough to guide himself. She was one of the main cornerstones upon which social work in Louisiana was built.

FRANCIS T. NICHOLLS

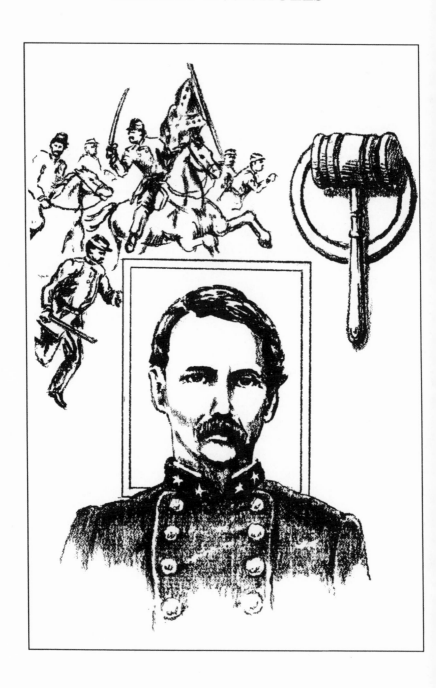

. . . the eye of the storm

IN THE QUIET BEND of the Mississippi River that is called Donaldsonville, in the zenith of a Louisiana August, Francis T. Nicholls was born over one hundred fifty years ago. He was the youngest of eight accomplished children, who, with the exception of Francis, died before their time either of war or of pestilence. The Nicholls family were descended from the gentry of sea-swept Cornwall, England. Edward Nicholls, their grandfather, was ordered by his family to study for the priesthood in a monastery in England. In time, the monastery was dissolved, and young Edward went to Paris. Disowned for disobedience, Edward migrated to Maryland, then Louisiana, thus establishing the American branch of the Nicholls family tree. Flamboyant lawyer, confidant to Gov. William C. C. Claiborne, here he stayed to his death.

Francis was the son of Thomas Nicholls, a veteran of the battle of New Orleans who later became a district judge. His mother, Louisa Drake Nicholls, was a published poetess. Her ancestors fought with the Colonials in the American Revolution. The blood of both soldier and dreamer mixed well in his veins, for Francis was both civil servant and visionary.

Francis Nicholls was a man who liked to watch the sun rise as he said his morning prayers. He read voraciously as a youngster and performed well in his studies. He was the first young man from Ascension Parish to gain entrance into West Point. He was given a commission in the elite artillery of the United States army as a lieutenant after graduating in 1855. But young Francis was sickened by the Indian wars he fought in. After serving in both Florida and California, he submitted his resignation following one year. He came home to Louisiana.

Like his father and grandfather, Francis wished to become a lawyer. His fondest dream was to one day be appointed judge. He entered the University of Louisiana, later to be known as Tulane University, and began his legal studies. He passed the board examination in 1858, and returned to Donaldsonville to practice law there and in neighboring Napoleonville.

In 1860 Francis Nicholls grasped the nettle of life and took unto him a wife. Caroline Guion, daughter of a judge in LaFourche Parish, was a darkly fragile, gaminlike creature. Unlike marriages between wealthy families of that period, the union of Francis and Caroline Nicholls was not prearranged by either family: It was based on mutual love and was a marriage of vast emotional depth, devotion, and commitment.

The hot-headed slogans of secession, that is, the South splitting away from the Union because of slavery, had little appeal for the level-headed, sensitive Francis. His family owned no slaves, and the three servants who were given to Caroline as a wedding gift were immediately granted their freedom by the young couple. Yet, when the state finally voted to secede from the Union in January 1861, like Robert E. Lee, Francis found he could not bear arms against his native state. He joined the Louisiana 8th Regiment and Lieutenant Colonel Nicholls served his regiment and new government well.

The Louisiana regiment received its baptism into the molten waters of war at the Battle of Bull Run. By 1862, the regiment, with men mainly from Ascension and Assumption Parishes, had become part of

106

Stonewall Jackson's legendary Shenandoah Campaign. In Winchester, Virginia, deep in the Shenandoah Valley, Francis Nicholls was seriously wounded in the left arm. Amputation, the only war-time cure for severe wounds to arms and legs, was performed. The Confederate army left Winchester and Francis, and the blue army of the North moved in, taking him prisoner as he lay recovering from this ordeal.

He was exchanged in September 1862, and the Confederate army assigned him to the field of battle once more. He was promoted to the rank of brigadier general in October 1862.

Seven months later, on a night in May that would see Gen. Stonewall Jackson shot by his own men, Francis was wounded again. Struck by a cannonball that traveled through the belly of his unfortunate horse and then severed his foot, he was once more maimed by the war.

Finally, he had not much more of his body to give to his country, the Confederate government placed him as a superintendent of the Conscript Bureau of the Trans-Mississippi Department until the end of the war in 1865.

Crippled in the prime of his life, Francis returned home to Louisiana and Reconstruction. He was now penniless. His boyhood home had been destroyed by the bombardment of Adm. David Farragut as he trekked through the waters of the Mississippi like an ironclad piranha, hell-bent on forcing Louisiana back into the Union. He and Caroline suffered the humiliation that the Yankee government inflicted on the conquered people of the state, especially the officers of the Rebel army. The degree of devastation throughout the South showed everyone that the Federal government meant business.

Even if it was dirty business.

Louisiana was immobilized by Reconstruction and the "Carpetbag" Regime. The notorious Returning Board ignored the candidates Louisianians elected into power and placed their own choices in positions of leadership. The Returning Board placed Republican misfits and undesirables into public office, doing its best to slap the faces of the people of Louisiana who had dared secede from the Union.

The very qualities that made Francis Nicholls quiet by nature, calm and reasoning, also instilled in him no desire for public life. Yet these same qualities were getting him noticed by the Democrats. They needed a person possessed of sterling qualities who could be the battering ram against the hated Carpetbagger Regime. By the time the governor's election of 1876 was at hand, they wanted Francis Nicholls as their man. At the state nominating convention, Sen. F. W. Goode of Terrebonne Parish announced to the assembly: "Gentlemen, I nominate all that is left of Gen. Francis T. Nicholls, for all that is left is right."

Nicholls defeated his opponent, S. B. Packard, soundly. He ignored the Returning Board's claim that Packard was governor and proceeded with his own inauguration. He established a de facto government, combining the three branches of the state government. With brilliant judgment, he used the system to beat the system. The presidential election had coincided with the governor's election, and Louisiana's electoral votes were the deciding factor in determining the nation's next president. President Ulysses Grant wanted fellow Republican Rutherford B. Hayes to succeed him. Francis Nicholls and the Democratic party in Louisiana filibustered for the delay of the counting of the state's electoral votes. The selection of the next president was held virtually hostage as a result of this action. When the time of the president's inauguration drew near, and the United States still had no named leader, Nicholls was promised the following if the filibuster was stopped: He would be recognized as the true governor, and S. B. Packard and all Federal troops would be withdrawn from Louisiana soil for good. The filibuster was stopped, the electoral votes counted. On April 26, 1877, Pres. Rutherford B. Hayes ordered all Federal troops out of Louisiana. Governor Nicholls, bayou lawyer, defeated Confederate, handicapped war veteran, had stared down the Federal government and delivered his home state from the illegal morass of Reconstruction.

The State capitol, at the beginning of his term as governor, was housed in the old St. Louis Hotel which is presently the site of the Royal Orleans Hotel. It was flanked by two barrooms, infamous watering holes which played havoc with the legislative sessions. Whether this was caused by drunken customers wandering into the legislature, or legislators wandering into the barrooms is difficult to pinpoint. However, the state capitol was moved to a more appropriate and less diverting location in Baton Rouge, where it remains to this day.

After seeing the seeds of his labors coming to fruition in the healing of Louisiana, Nicholls returned to the quiet of family life and law practice.

In 1888, he was re-elected governor and found himself involved in yet another standoff. The Louisiana Lottery was seeking extension of its charter. Refusing lottery officials' bribes, he vetoed the bill extending the lottery's charter as soon as it passed the legislature. All of the plotting of the lottery officials was foiled by the penstroke of one honest man.

Like King Arthur of English legend, he used his power as governor in the spirit of "might for right."

He coolly cleaned out Carpetbagger corruption in every part of state government. Appointing to his cabinet men of honor and competence, which also included a black man, he began to turn his idealistic dreams of reform into reality. Perhaps remembering the loss of two beloved sisters to yellow fever, he updated and improved the Public Health system. Perhaps remembering the devastation of his neighbors' property due to the rampaging Mississippi, he saw to the modernization of the levee system and was awarded the control of the Mississippi when it becomes furious in the spring. Having known hardship, he sold undeveloped land near Crowley to struggling war veterans and widows, charging hardly any money, and brought in agricultural experts to assist these new landowners in farming. Thus began the flourishing bounty of Louisiana's rice lands. He strove to attain racial balance in the society of Louisiana. Under his guidance, Louisiana began to settle its once topsy-turvy axis. Perhaps even more important, Nicholls was writing a new chapter in the recovery of lost human dignity for people of his state.

Nicholls kept vigilant watch over his state. He saw to the establishment and propagation of the American Society for the Prevention of Cruelty to Animals in Louisiana. School textbooks were required to contain at least one chapter explaining the effects and dangers of alcohol and drugs.

In 1892, as his second term ended, he was rewarded his lifelong dream: He was named a judge. Chief Justice Francis T. Nicholls of the Louisiana Supreme Court served on this bench, a wise Solomon, for the next nineteen years.

And then, failing health prompted his retirement. He left New Orleans and his judgeship and returned home, back to the halcyon cadence of life as it existed beside the "father of waters" as it flowed homeward to the freedom of the sea. In his plantation near Thibodaux, on a luminous green-gold day in January 1912, Francis Nicholls quietly died.

In the annals of Louisiana history, the story of Governor Nicholls is perhaps one of the most shimmering. He was a generous leader grateful for the trust placed in him by the people of Louisiana.

He was beloved by black and white alike, and in a state that is nearly three hundred years old, he is considered to be the most heroic of its figures.

ELIZA NICHOLSON

. . . womanhood

SHE WAS CONSIDERED, by her family, *the* Poitevants of Pearlington, Mississippi, to be a shy and gentle blossom on the frail tree of Southern womanhood.
Eliza Jane Poitevant, born March 11, 1849, was a
dreamy girl who was raised by one of her aunts because of her mother's flimsy health. As a young girl,
instead of listening to her lessons, she wrote poetry
during classroom hours. She seemed unable to keep
her mind focused on mathematics and away from the
beauty of the woods and river outside where she
longed to wander. But her inability to stop daydream-
ing didn't seem to hurt her. The poetry produced by
her dreams was published in both New York and New
Orleans. Eliza published under the name "Pearl
Rivers" as a tribute to the abiding love she had for the
Pearl River that flowed past her family's plantation.

Eliza Jane grew up in the hoop-skirted, pampered,
and courtly society of the antebellum South, and survived the ravages of the Civil War and Reconstruction.
When she was only twenty-one years old, the New
Orleans *Picayune* newspaper offered her a position as
literary editor. The paper was named after a coin, the
picayune, which was the price of one issue. The year
was 1870, and New Orleans from the standpoint of
the Poitevants, was infested with the Union troops
occupying the city. What's more, the state of Louisiana fairly reeked with the rottenness of the corrupt
Carpetbagger regime that was in power. To the delicate horror of her French Huguenot family, their Eliza
shamefully revealed to the world that she had intelligence and talent that went beyond just appearing

113

decorative in a parlor. She accepted the *Picayune's* offer, left the sheltering bosom of her family, and moved to New Orleans. It was unheard of conduct for a lady in those days.

Eliza brought her rustling, sachet-scented skirts to a world inhabited by men—a world of ink, paper, words, and print deadlines. She worked for a newspaper that was mainly written with male readers in mind. Her face, demure and mischievous, along with her intelligence, caught the attention of Col. A. M. Holbrook, the newspaper's owner. Two years after Eliza joined the staff of the paper, she and Colonel Holbrook married. Eliza had a hair-raising experience when the colonel's ex-wife came to New Orleans and tried to murder her. Spunky Eliza survived the threat to her life without injury, and she and the colonel published their paper together. But the colonel, already elderly, died when his new bride was only twenty-six.

In 1876, Eliza inherited the paper from her husband. Although it was one of the most widely read periodicals in the South, Colonel Holbrook's mismanagement had the *Picayune* knee-deep in debt. In addition to the debt, Eliza was dismayed to learn that several people were suing the paper.

Back in Mississippi, the Poitevants were begging their beloved, reserved Eliza to return her mass of auburn hair and clear blue eyes to her family and to genteelly grieve out her widowhood in decorous mourning. But Eliza didn't pick up her skirts and run back home. Instead, she picked up the burden of a debt-ridden daily that needed a responsible publisher. She became its chief executive and, with the aid of a devoted staff, began to turn the tide in favor of the *Picayune*.

When she announced to the public that she would

run the newspaper, Eliza declared that it would be a periodical for the people and not politicians. She further stated that while it was proudly a Southern newspaper, it would never support any fanatical Southern beliefs of secession.

With the help of George Nicholson, her business manager, Eliza dragged her publication from the mire of debt. On June 27, 1878, she and George were married. Since George's talents lay in finances, Eliza could trust money matters to him and devote herself to the imaginative part of publishing. She expanded the male-oriented *Picayune* by printing news and columns for both women and children. This included a children's department as well as columns on fashion, health, and efficient housekeeping. She opened business and job opportunities for women by hiring female journalists. She successfully handled being a wife, the mother of two sons, and the first woman publisher of a major newspaper in the United States. In 1884, she was elected president of the Women's National Press Association. The New York Women's Press Club chose Eliza as its first honorary member.

Of understated elegance, Eliza was also softhearted and championed many social causes. But it was her ardent love for defenseless animals that made her an almost militant trailblazer who was one of the founders of the American Society for the Prevention of the Cruelty to Animals in New Orleans. And still, poetry, fairy tales, stories, and theater talk flowed from the pen of "Pearl Rivers" and found their way in other publications across the nation.

The family she left behind in Mississippi who regretted her "unwomanly" behavior hopefully realized just how much of a woman their Eliza was. She nursed a dying newspaper back to life, saving countless jobs for its employees. She was loving and gentle enough to insist on humane treatment for both the under-privileged and for helpless animals. She had the courage to compete with disapproving men and win. She was a flower of the Old South who chose not to die after its first blossoming, but rather to bloom again and again in many different roles. That was the power of her creative force.

On February 15, 1896, Eliza Jane Poitevant Nicholson died during a flu epidemic. Her husband George died ten days before her. She was only forty-seven years old. Among her survivors were her two sons and the newspaper New Orleanians find on their doorstep each morning to this very day: *The Times-Picayune*.

ALTON OCHSNER

HE WAS CHRISTENED Edward William Alton Ochsner, born May 4, 1896, in a territory now known as South Dakota that was still fresh from the blood-bath of the Indian Wars. He was the only son of six children. Alton's father, Edward Philip Ochsner, had journeyed from Bear Valley, Wisconsin, in a covered wagon with his wife, Clara Leda, and their two little daughters. The year was 1879, and the unsettled South Dakota territory was a hazard of fearsome winters and even more fearsome Indian attacks. Rugged and beautiful, it was also a land where a man's spirit could be challenged and triumph. Edward blazed into the unknown. It was a spirit that would help turn his son into a medical legend. Nearly eighty years after his father left the security of Wisconsin for the wilds of South Dakota, Alton Ochsner would step into an operating room in September of 1953 in steamy Louisiana and perform the first successful surgical separation of Siamese twins in history.

The name Ochsner (pronounced Ox-ner) is German, meaning "herder of oxen." Alton Ochsner's ancestors came from Blicheim Benteingen County, Bagen, Germany, and the Alsace region of France.

Alton's father was a prosperous and prominent member of the small town of Kimball, South Dakota, who also served as the town's sheriff. As he grew up, the only son amid a household of females, Alton was both spoiled and disciplined. Surrounded as he was with barnyard animals and Shetland ponies, one of Alton's chores was to milk the cows daily.

In school, Alton was a very intelligent student. He

119

usually finished his schoolwork before the rest of his classmates. On Sundays, his family worshiped in their mother's Presbyterian faith. He was a good boy, but not above throwing a lit firecracker into a sleeping neighbor's bedroom with his good buddy Henry Bray one Fourth of July. When bored from schoolwork, the little boy read Horatio Alger.

In 1914, Alton left Kimball for the University of South Dakota at Vermillion and began pre-med studies. He maintained an almost perfect A average. He helped support himself by waiting tables at his fraternity house. When he received his Bachelor of Arts degree from the University of South Dakota, he went to Chicago where his cousin Albert, a brilliant surgeon, arranged an externship at the Augustana Hospital. Fascinated, Alton saw operations and learned the daily routines that help heal a patient. It was a relatively new world of surgery then. The importance of performing operations in germ-free surroundings had only been recently discovered. Nearly twenty years before, hand washing and antiseptics were laughed at by doctors who operated on patients or delivered babies maskless, in long black frock coats instead of surgical gowns, with hands that came unwashed straight from other sick patients. Alton was beginning his career as medicine was beginning its enlightened age. From Chicago, he went to the Washington University Medical School in St. Louis.

In autumn of 1922, Alton left the United States for Europe. He was to spend two years abroad—one year in Germany studying under one of the greatest surgeons of the Continent, Prof. Victor Schmedier of the University of Frankfurt, and for another year in Switzerland with the other greatest surgeon of Europe, Prof. Paul Clairmon of the University of Zurich. Before leaving America, Alton had become engaged

120

to the pretty and dark-haired Miss Isabel Lockwood. Feeling torn between love and the career opportunity of a lifetime, Alton chose to go to Europe as long as Isabel would join him after one year, at which time they would be married. Alton was kept busy and before he knew it, it was September 1923 and time for him to become a married man. Isabel sailed from America, and the day after her arrival they were married in Zurich, Switzerland. One year later, Alton and a very pregnant Isabel were on a return voyage to America. Isabel went into premature labor, and in the ship's infirmary, in the middle of the Atlantic Ocean, she delivered her first child and named him for his father. The three Ochsners returned to an America deep in prohibition, where flappers danced the Charleston to jazz music and sipped illegal gin. In 1926, because of his love for teaching, Alton became an assistant professor of surgery at the University of Wisconsin in Madison. Within one year, he had discovered a foolproof and easy method of treating a sometimes fatal disease of the bronchial tubes, common in Wisconsin because of the harsh winters.

In 1927, his name was submitted as a nominee to become chairman of the Department of Surgery at Tulane Medical School in New Orleans. He was only thirty years old. He impressed the medical school's staff so much that he was offered the position.

Growing a mustache in the hope that it would add maturity to his young face, Alton came to New Orleans. For the next thirteen years he slaved in his new position. But he liked New Orleans. The small-town boy of South Dakota, who would one day reign as Rex on Mardi Gras Day, happily adapted himself to the customs of the city.

In 1940, Alton and five other doctors banded together to form a clinic that would allow them to see patients and earn money in addition to teaching. It was a revolutionary idea. When they received financial backing for the plan, other doctors of New Orleans were distressed almost to the point of militarism. Feeling betrayed, they sent Alton and his comrades a gift one Holy Thursday night: a tiny leather pouch holding thirty silver dimes and a note which told them that the thirty pieces of silver were donations for their clinic from the dentists and medical doctors of New Orleans.

The five "Judases" named Alton as the head of the clinic, and then christened it with his name. The clinic grew into a massive medical center, on Jefferson Highway, by the banks of the Mississippi River.

Alton pressed on in his career in his father's pioneer spirit. He performed surgery on governors, heads of state, actors such as Gary Cooper, Argentine dictator Juan Peron, and golfer Ben Hogan in addition to the poverty-stricken residents of the United States and South America he welcomed to his medical foundation.

Alton probably won the eternal wrath of the tobacco industry when he was the first physician to show to the world that smoking caused lung cancer and was to be avoided. He led a movement to stamp out smoking because he was sickened by extreme suffering *and* death the habit caused. Smoking was thought to be a harmless habit until Alton proved otherwise.

In 1968, Isabel, his wife, died. In time, Alton married Jane Kellogg Sturdy, who was devoted to him.

Before his death in September 1981, he had received every honor that can be bestowed upon a physician. He had taught countless young doctors and cured countless patients. His surgical techniques were published in journals and textbooks and passed on to students and physicians throughout the world who used them to cure their own patients. Alton Ochsner perhaps never really knew just how many lives he actually helped save, nor how much suffering he eased. Lighting the medical world with his uncanny brilliance, he assured that his medical discoveries would be used long after his death, helping patients yet to be born, reaching deep into the frontier that is the future.

HENRY SHREVE

. . . the freedom of the rivers

HENRY MILLER SHREVE, born October 21, 1785, was the son of a Quaker named Israel. Israel, by breaking his church's anti-war belief because he fought in the Revolutionary War alongside George Washington, had gotten into considerable hot water with Quaker church elders. When Henry was two years old, his father took his entire family away from the New Jersey frontier that had been their home and settled near the Youghiogheny River in southwestern Pennsylvania. Henry was the youngest child, but made himself useful to his family as he explored the fields and woods near his home. By trapping rabbits, he helped bring food to the family's table; climbing trees, he picked the fruit his mother and sisters would cook into jams and preserves.

Henry lived in an area rich with inland rivers that were fed by the tumbling waters of creeks, streams, and runs. The well-traveled Youghiogheny River was jammed with flatboats that carried supplies headed for hilly Pittsburgh. Families, looking for new homesteads, crowded children, livestock, furnishings, and overland wagons onto the flatboats and drifted down the water's currents. Henry came to love the river and spent hours watching the bustle of the life it led. The flowing waters fed the flowing new life in America, and Henry came to respect the importance of the river when he was very young.

When he became older and could be spared from his chores, young Henry was allowed to take part in the building of a flatboat. Sometimes Henry was allowed to whittle the oaken pegs that helped hold the flatboat together.

By the year 1799, Henry's father was in terrible health, as was his friend and former commander, George Washington. When both Israel Shreve and George Washington died on the same day, December 14, 1799, Henry was barely fourteen. His father's money problems did not leave his family in too secure a financial position. Henry went to work as a riverboatman and sailed the length of the nation down to New Orleans. He traveled the rivers on flatboats that passed forests wherein Indians silently stood among the trees, watching. Henry met Canadian woodsmen, whose boat keels were piled with beaver pelts. There on the river, Henry grew to be tall, with wavy brown hair and eyes that were as grey as a rainy day. By the time he was twenty-two, he had earned enough money to buy his own keelboat and had learned enough to become a commercial navigator.

As much as Henry loved his work poling downriver to a destination, returning home to Pennsylvania was sheer agony. In order for a flatboat to travel *upriver*, it was necessary to use a system called *cordelling*. A stout rope, or *cordelle*, a thousand feet long was attached to the mast of the boat. The crew would swim to shore with the rope and then pull the boat upriver by their own strength. Walking over pathways of rocks, hills and oozing mud, they'd pull the boats up the Mississippi and Ohio Rivers to reach Pennsylvania. Dragging a boat from New Orleans to Pittsburgh against bounding river currents was no easy task, but Henry succeeded and prospered. In 1811, he was secure enough in his financial position to marry Miss Mary Blair and become the father of a baby girl. He traded furs, delivered cargo to New Orleans, and bought a larger barge that could also carry passengers. Now, if only he could find a better system than cordelling so he could return home faster to his bride.

But cordelling was his lot until deliverance came in the form of Robert Fulton's new invention. The first Mississippi River steamboat, the *New Orleans,* was a magnificent craft with a giant hull painted slate blue. Its beautiful paddlewheels spun like kaleidoscopes. What's more, it could travel upriver on steampower, not manpower. Henry began studying the *New Orleans'* progress and its problems.

By 1813, he had his own steamship built and called it the *Enterprise.* It was the first steamship ever to complete a round trip from New Orleans to Louisville, Kentucky. Two years earlier, the New Madrid fault had awakened from its long sleep and caused many earthquakes that changed the course of the Mississippi and created new lakes on the face of the earth. But still Henry navigated the waters. The more he learned about the Mississippi River, the more he realized he still did not know. By 1814, as New Orleans prepared to defend itself against the British, Henry slipped the *Enterprise* past the English ships blocking the harbor and delivered crucial military supplies to Gen. Andrew Jackson for the defense of the city.

Always studying boat design, Henry soon built the *George Washington.* It was a lush floating hotel and cargo carrier. Its unique design proved to be the perfect vessel for traveling the river. Other riverboat owners copied Henry's design and built their own boats modeled after the *George Washington.* And so, commerce and trade boomed on the Mississippi and fed the income of New Orleans and Louisiana.

In 1827, Pres. John Adams appointed Henry superintendent of river improvement in the West. Henry invented the "snagboat," which was actually two boats fastened together and equipped with a machine that sawed away logs and other snarls underwater. It was operated by men on board who constantly turned the machine's wheel. It had cleared the Ohio River and made it safe to navigate.

Northern Louisiana was impossible to reach except by an unbearable overland journey that made populating the area out of the question. Although the Red River cut clearly across Louisiana from the Northwest to join hands with the Mississippi, it was clogged with driftwood, sand, and logs that made it impassable. This great Red River "raft" reached 160 miles above Natchitoches and was an enormous snag cutting the state in two. Using the snagboat, Henry began work to clear the Great Raft and finally succeeded in 1841. The whole of Louisiana was an open door from the Gulf of Mexico to the piney Northern bluffs. In a log home at Bennett's Bluff, Henry Shreve opened a store and trading post. The river he had cleared helped give birth to a city that grew around the site of his camp. Settlers who came up the mahogany waters of the Red River christened their town with the name of its father: Shreveport.

Henry's first wife, Mary, died, and he married a lady from Boston named Lydia Rogers. Henry died on his plantation in Missouri on March 6, 1851. His innovation and stamina unblocked the heart of the new nation and gave to America the freedom of its rivers. Although he was born far from Louisiana, the years of his sweat and ceaseless toil that helped connect north with south in the state clearly bestow upon him the name of native son.

JUDAH TOURO

LONG BEFORE QUEEN ISABELLA of Spain sent Christopher Columbus to search for his new world, the ancestors of Judah Touro had settled in Spain and Portugal. They were Jewish, and therefore were known as the "Sephardim." This was a name given to Jews of Spanish and Portuguese blood. The Sephardic people not expelled from these two countries because of their religion became known as "Marranos," or "Accursed Ones." They were forced to become Christians if they wished to avoid exile. Discovered practicing Judaism secretly, the Marranos were burned at the stake in what amounted to mass murder.

Most of the other European countries also persecuted the Jews, and there was no safe place for them.

Except for the Netherlands. The Dutch rebelled against Spain and won their independence. The Netherlands opened wide its gates to the Sephardim. From hooded monks, chains, dungeons, and the screams of the dying, Judah Touro's ancestors went to Holland. There were beautiful windmills spinning in their own breeze, fields filled with flowers spreading in all colors of the spectrum, and cooled by soft winds that blew from the surrounding zees. The Touros became beloved and wealthy citizens of Holland. After persecution and exile, they found their own land of milk and honey there.

Judah's father, Isaac, was born in Amsterdam in 1738. A fine merchant, Isaac was also the *Hazan,* or cantor, of his temple. A large group of the Sephardim, due to the settling of the Dutch in the eastern part of America, lived in Newport, Rhode Island. Isaac Touro joined them. Fifteen years after his arrival, he married Regina Hays. The second of their three children, Judah, was born on June 16, 1775. In the beginning of the Revolutionary War, Newport was occupied by the British. The Touro family had to evacuate the town and joined relatives in Kingston, Jamaica.

When Isaac died in the West Indies in 1784, Regina returned to New England. She and her children lived with her brother, Michael Moses Hayes, and his family in Boston.

Judah's Uncle Moses was a warm, kindly man, generous to both beggars and prominent citizens, Christians and Jews. During the War for Independence, he was a patriotic supporter of the Revolution. He thrilled to the new doctrines of liberty scribed in the Declaration of Independence, especially the herald's blast that sounded for religious freedom. When Judah's mother died, Moses lovingly raised him as a son and trained him to be a sound merchant. But on one vital issue they were never to agree, and that was Moses' daughter, Catherine.

Judah and Catherine, growing up together in the same house, had been inseparable. On becoming man and woman, they had fallen deeply in love. Wanting to hurry the day when they would forget all about one another, Moses sent twenty-three-year-old Judah on a long voyage to the Mediterranean to handle a shipping matter for him. Napoleon's wars were tearing Europe apart, and the journey would be a dangerous one. During the voyage, Judah's ship was attacked by French pirates. Judah fought courageously, and got his cargo safely to its destination. When he returned to Boston, if he thought his bravery would allow him

132

to claim the hand of the fair Catherine, he was mistaken. Three years later, Moses sent him from his home and employ. Judah and Catherine would never meet again. And to the end of their days, they never forgot one another. They both remained single for the rest of their lives.

Judah went, at first, to Boston, then left for New Orleans in 1801. It was practically a frontier river town, yet the port of New Orleans was thriving, its commerce growing larger each day. Judah arrived in New Orleans in February 1802. It was a city under French rule, and very naughty. New Orleans had no street lights. The people had to roam the streets after dark with lanterns in their hands if they weren't to become lost. The population was close to eight thousand and English was hardly spoken.

Aided by his fine reputation as a businessman, Judah established a store. The Jewish New Englander, with true Yankee thrift, began to succeed in his business. Adopting Louisiana as his home, he became a Southerner in his heart.

The ongoing war in Europe was ruining American shipping commerce. European ports were impossible for American vessels to reach. New England merchants, burdened with an extra supply of goods with no one to sell them to, looked to Judah and the port of New Orleans for a possible solution for the sales of their products. By 1810, the vast shipping trade of New England sent every sailing vessel with merchandise only to Judah. Not only did Judah's personal income grow by leaps and bounds, but his honesty gave the port of New Orleans the reputation of being an excellent location for the distribution of merchandise. New Orleans soon rivaled New York, Liverpool, and London as a port. The curves of the Mississippi were filled with tall ships and schooners, the brilliance of their sails flashing in the daylight. The port was alive with the sound of wooden ships creaking and masts beating together in the wind that hummed through the sails. The perfume of coffee, West Indian spices, and dampened wood were called forth by the yellow tropical sun, and rode on the humid Louisiana air.

Purchasing steamers, Judah gave the economy of New Orleans another shot in the arm by helping to introduce the valued paddlewheelers to the shipping industry.

His fame in business was widespread; his fame as a philanthropist came later, and only after his supreme efforts to hide it began to fail.

When the British began nearing the city to take it from America at the close of 1814, Judah abandoned his trade and joined the state militia. A piece of a twelve-pound shot struck Judah in the thigh and for twelve months he lay bedridden.

Once he recovered, he returned to his work and charitable deeds. Judah quietly made donations to establish hospitals and almshouses in Jerusalem. He assisted the persecuted Jews in China. In New Orleans, the Hebrew Benevolent Society, and the Israelite Society for the Relief of the Sick also benefited from his generosity. He financed the construction of the first free library in New Orleans himself.

When Palestine missionaries arrived in New Orleans seeking assistance for the Christians who were being persecuted in Jerusalem, they were sent to see Judah Touro. The Jewish man donated more to their work than any Christian in New Orleans. Judah's financial help also kept the Christian First Congregational Church from extinction.

With his adopted city crippled by yellow fever epidemics nearly every summer, Judah founded a hospital for the treatment of its victims. And Touro Infirmary exists to this day, one of the largest medical centers in the South. He helped establish synagogues in New Orleans and united his Hebrew brethren. His own conduct won respect and understanding for the Jews themselves. He bought slaves just so he could immediately free them, or hired them as employees.

Two weeks before his death in January 1854, Judah bequeathed his large fortune to a few friends and to nearly thirty charitable organizations throughout the world. Unknown to him, his beloved Catherine had died a few days before he wrote his will. In the fever of the last days of his illness, he talked about walking in a garden with Catherine.

He could not be considered a handsome man by any stretch of the imagination. His eyebrows were too bushy, his mouth somewhat lopsided, and the large stovepipe hat he always wore sometimes pushed his ears down and outward, making them look like wings. He was a proper, shy, and grumpy looking elderly man.

Yet he was one of the most beloved citizens of New Orleans. Shrewd and keen in business, he was forever soft-hearted to the needs of others.

After his death, perhaps Judah won the prize he so greatly wished for in life, and perhaps, somewhere, he walks with his beloved Catherine in a garden.

135

SOPHIE B. WRIGHT

SHE LOOKED MORE like a heroine of a fairy tale than a person who toiled for the betterment of society. Dainty, small, and delicate, her eyes were as large, light, and clear as sea water, her hairy as wavy. Born in 1866, one year after the end of the Civil War, Sophie and her parents were made paupers because of the Southern defeat. Their family had been planters who lost everything, and Sophie's father was ill equipped to make a decent living for his wife and child in post-war New Orleans.

When Sophie was three years old, she suffered a terrible fall that injured her back and hips, crippling her for life. Although she was poverty-stricken and handicapped, Sophie's wise Scottish mother did not encourage self-pity in her little daughter, nor did she spoil her. Instead, she helped Sophie fight against feeling helpless by teaching her to do whatever she could to help others. Mrs. Wright also made certain that her little girl was educated and sent her to public school when Sophie was nine years old.

At the end of five years, the public education system had taught Sophie all it could. Sophie was a sweet-tempered fourteen-year-old, but she also had the spirit of a crusader. With her hair still in pigtails, and not being quite old enough yet to wear long skirts, Sophie Bell Wright started her own school.

Filling a room in her family's cottage with benches borrowed from a public school and hanging a shingle on her front door that read "DAY SCHOOL FOR GIRLS," the young girl started her classes with one pupil in attendance. She charged fifty cents per month for each student. At the end of the first year, Sophie's cottage school was filled with twenty young ladies, and its tiny, pinafored school mistress was happily contributing the glorious sum of ten dollars a month to help her family. And so, while the family's dinner simmered in a pot on the kitchen stove, and outside the family's wash flapped on a clothesline drying in warm golden sunlight, Miss Sophie, with crutches, educated her roomful of young girls.

She did her job of teaching so well that soon her students were advancing past their teacher. When she was sixteen, Sophie realized that she would need more education herself if she were to remain a competent educator. Visiting the principal of a school with an advanced curriculum, she impressed him with her knowledge of mathematics. He agreed to teach her languages as payment if she taught math to beginners at his school. With mornings spent teaching at her own school, and the rest of the day finding her both teacher and student, Sophie was a busy young lady.

The young people of the city began flocking to her to learn. Her family's cottage was no longer large enough to hold all of her students. At age eighteen, Sophie arranged for a loan to pay rent on a larger house. By the end of the first year, the loan was repaid and her new school was a complete success.

The underprivileged children of New Orleans had few champions to fight for them during the 1800s. The second half of the nineteenth century brought into New Orleans more factories, foundries, and mills that used child labor. Working long hours daily for only pennies, little boys and girls weren't protected by any law that insisted they be educated instead of employed. And their ignorance would always hold them back and keep them downtrodden in a dead-end way of life.

The evening a twenty-five-year-old man knocked at the door of the Day School for Girls helped change the course of education in New Orleans forever. Seeking schooling to help him find a better job, he asked Sophie if she would teach him at night when he finished working during the day at a menial job. Kind-hearted Sophie didn't refuse him. Night after night, he came to her to be taught in the dim light of a kerosene lamp. It wasn't long before he brought friends with him, and then, by word of mouth, other young men joined them until Sophie had to recruit volunteers to help with the night classes. She had only two requirements for a young man's admission to her school: He must have regular employment during daylight hours, and he must be *unable* to afford tuition. It was the beginning of the first free night school in New Orleans.

Her school grew even more, and the "Home Institute" was in need of larger quarters. Thinking of the young people sweating in the mills and factories, she found a house on Camp Street and opened a school near the city's rough industrial section. She obtained more books, added more teachers, and made another large loan to cover expenses.

Only the yellow fever epidemic of 1897 took Sophie from her dedication to teaching. New Orleans was again stricken by the disease, and the city closed down. Sophie turned her school into a warehouse to receive medical supplies, food, and clothing. Taking her teaching staff with her, she went out into the disease-infested streets of New Orleans and distributed her comforting supplies to the sick.

The closing of the school meant that her payments

on the loan couldn't be met. As she worked to help yellow fever victims, hobbling on crutches through the humid night air that turned her wavy hair to ringlets and wilted the starch in her shirtwaist, she was steeling herself to realize that she would probably lose her school. But when the fever at last left New Orleans, a banker who respected Sophie and admired her tremendous work, paid off the entire debt and then loaned her an additional ten thousand dollars to improve her school.

By 1903, Sophie was forced to turn away three hundred applicants. Her students were over fifteen hundred strong with forty teachers on her staff. She opened the night school to girls and added algebra, calculus, shorthand, and bookkeeping to the curriculum. She hired teachers who spoke languages other than English, thereby helping foreign students who had immigrated to America learn more effectively. In addition to teaching, Sophie served as president of the Home for the Incurables.

In the early 1900s, Sophie was the first person ever to receive the *Picayune* newspaper's Loving Cup, an award to the person in New Orleans considered to be its finest citizen of the year. It was awarded to her at Audubon Park and handed to her by her overjoyed students.

The quality of life in a city is the direct result of the quality of its citizens. Sophie Bell Wright realized that personal enlightenment in one person can spread and enlighten others. Crippled, racked by asthma, she still aided thousands of poor children realize their potential. Informed and trained by her school, these children escaped the sweat shops and mills to find better ways of living. Enlightenment of people caused the end of the child labor and brought about more humane labor laws. And the influence of a young crippled girl set a standard in Louisiana's public education that would be followed for generations.

In 1912, Sophie Wright died. While she lived it was often written about her that she was living "the most beautiful life in New Orleans."

BIBLIOGRAPHY

BOOKS

Allan, William. *The Life and Work of John McDonogh.* Metairie, Louisiana: Jefferson Parish Historical Commission, 1983.

Allen, Maury. *Ron Guidry, Louisiana Lightnin'.* New York, New York: Harvey House, 1979.

Bush, Robert. *Grace King: A Southern Destiny.* Baton Rouge, Louisiana: Louisiana State University Press, 1983.

Carter, Doris Dorcas. *Charles P. Adams and Grambling College.* Thesis, Louisiana Tech University, 1971, Ann Arbor, Michigan: The University of Michigan Microfilms, 1980.

Casso, Evans J. *Francis T. Nicholls: A Biographical Tribute.* Thibodaux, Louisiana: Nicholls College Foundation, 1987.

Chase, John Churchill. *Frenchmen, Desire, Good Children.* New York, New York: Collier Books, 1949.

Collier, James Lincoln. *Louis Armstrong, An American Genius.* New York, New York: Oxford University Press, 1983.

Dubroca, Isabella. *Good Neighbor Eleanor McMain of Kingsley House.* New Orleans, Louisiana: Pelican Publishing Company, 1955.

Frost, Orcutt William. *The Early Life of Lafcadio Hearn.* Thesis, University of Illinois, Ann Arbor, Michigan: The University of Michigan Microfilms, 1977.

Gallott, Mildred. *A History of Grambling State University.* Lanham, Maryland: University Press of America, 1985.

Garvey, Joan and Mary Lou Widmer. *Beautiful Crescent.* New Orleans, Louisiana: Garmer Press, 1982.

Gayarré, Charles. *History of Louisiana, Volumes II & III.* New Orleans, Louisiana: F. F. Hansell and Brothers, Ltd. 4th Edition, 1903.

Gehman, Mary and Nancy Ries. *Women and New Orleans: A History.* New Orleans, Louisiana: Margaret Media, Inc., 1985.

Giddins, Gary. *Satchmo.* New York, New York: Doubleday, 1988.

Greenfields: Two Hundred Years of Louisiana Sugar. The Center for Louisiana Studies, Lafayette, Louisiana: 1980.

Guyol, Louis Hubert. *A Center of Brightness: A History of the Pioneer Days of Kingsley House of New Orleans.* New Orleans, Louisiana: Published by Kingsley House of New Orleans and New Orleans Day Nursery Association, 1961.

Huhner, Leon. *The Life of Judah Touro.* Philadelphia, Pennsylvania: The Jewish Public Society of America, 1946.

Kirby, David K. *Grace King.* Boston, Massachusetts: Twayne's United States Authors Series, 1980.

McCall, Edith. *Conquering the River: Henry Miller Shreve and the Navigation of American Inland Waterways.* Baton Rouge: Louisiana, Louisiana State University Press, 1984.

McCarthy, Albert. *Louis Armstrong.* Cranberry, New Jersey: A.S. Barnes and Company, 1959.

Martinez, Raymond. *The Immortal Margaret Haughery.* New Orleans, Louisiana: Hope Publishing Company, 1967.

Matthews, John L. *Sophie Bell Wright: The Story of a Noble Life in Everyday Magazine,* n.p., n.d.

Rand, Clayton. *Stars in Their Eyes: Dreamers and Builders in Louisiana.* Gulfport, Mississippi: Dixie Press, 1953.

Reeves, Miriam. *The Governors of Louisiana*. Gretna, Louisiana: Pelican Press, 1976.

Romero, Sidney J. *"My Fellow Citizens. . ."*. The Inaugural Addresses of Louisiana Governors. Lafayette, Louisiana: The Center for Louisiana Studies.

Socola, Edward Magruder. *Charles Gayarré: A Biography*. Thesis, University of Pennsylvania, Ann Arbor, Michigan: The University of Michigan Microfilms, 1977.

Stevenson, Elizabeth. *Lafcadio Hearn*. New York, New York: MacMillan, 1961.

Thomas, Edward. *Lafcadio Hearn*. Boston, Massachusetts: Houghton Mifflin, 1912.

Wilds, John. *Alton Ochsner: Surgeon of the South*. Baton Rouge, Louisiana: Louisiana State University Press, 1990.

Wilds, John. *Ochsners': An Informal History of the South's Largest Medical Center*. Baton Rouge, Louisiana: Louisiana State University Press, 1985.

Williams, T. Harry. *Huey Long*. New York, New York: Random House, 1969.

Wilson, James L. *Clementine Hunter, American Folk Artist*. Gretna, Louisiana: Pelican Publishing, 1988.

Yu, Beogcheon. *An Ape of Gods: The Art and Thought of Lafcadio Hearn*. Detroit, Michigan: Wayne State University Press, 1964.

Zimman, David. *The Day Huey Long Died*. Obolensky, Inc., USA, 1963.

NEWSPAPER ARTICLE

Anonymous author, "Captain Cooley, Veteran Master of Packets, Dies," New Orleans *Times-Picayune*, December 20, 1931.